THE TRIUMPH OF TIME

THE TRIUMPH OF TIME

*A Study of the Victorian Concepts
of Time, History, Progress,
and Decadence*

***

Jerome Hamilton Buckley

THE BELKNAP PRESS OF
HARVARD UNIVERSITY PRESS
Cambridge, Massachusetts
1 9 6 6

© Copyright 1966 by the President and Fellows of Harvard College

Distributed in Great Britain by Oxford University Press, London

Library of Congress Catalog Card Number 66–21333

Printed in the United States of America

TO
WALTER JACKSON BATE

PREFACE

"The 'spirit of the age,'" wrote John Stuart Mill on the eve of the Victorian era, "is in some measure a novel expression. I do not believe that it is to be met with in any work exceeding fifty years in antiquity. The idea of comparing one's own age with former ages, or with our notion of those which are yet to come, had occurred to philosophers; but it never before was itself the dominant idea of any age." Indeed, he continued, the idea could take hold only in such an age of rapid and decisive change as the nineteenth century self-consciously recognized itself to be. "Before men begin to think much and long on the peculiarities of their own times, they must have begun to think that those times are, or are destined to be, distinguished in a very remarkable manner from the times that preceded them. Mankind are then divided, into those who are still what they were, and those who have changed: into the men of the present age, and the men of the past. To the former, the spirit of the age is a subject of exultation; to the latter, of terror; to both, of eager and anxious interest."[1]

The present book sets out not to chart afresh the spirit of the Victorian age, but simply to test the truth of Mill's suggestion that his own generation had a quite unprecedented awareness of time, and of itself in time, and a will to view the course of history with "eager and anxious interest"—with either the exultation that accompanies the idea of progress or the terror that attends the assumption of decadence. It attempts to describe a multiple concern with time, both public and private. "Public time," as I use the label, involves the attitudes of the society as a living changing whole, the *Zeitgeist*, as Mill understood it, the general preoccupation with the upward or downward movement of the "times," and the commitment to the contemporary. "Private time," on the other hand, relates to the subjective experience of the individual, his memories of a personal past, his will to accept or oppose the demands of the public present, and finally his effort to conquer time, to escape from the tyranny of the temporal, to find beyond the flux of things some token of stability.

My study is primarily Victorian in reference, though it ranges frequently back to the early nineteenth century, when *Zeitgeist* first became "the dominant idea," and forward into the early twentieth, where the preoccupation with time continued unabated. And it is for the most part literary in its sources, though it undertakes no detailed analysis of the literary techniques of registering time's passage or quality. The author of a recent social history of Victorian England argues persuasively that as historian he must "try to disregard a little that self-conscious, self-confident minority who seem to have made history and certainly have normally written about it, whose voices, unless we are careful, are the only ones we are likely to hear from the past."[2] But the student of literary history or the history of ideas, working as he does with expressed thought and emotion, must necessarily, I believe, give little attention to the inarticulate majority, far less, for instance, to the wordless millions than to the Matthew Arnold who perceived their condition. He must heed first and last, it seems to me, the familiar, sensitive, self-conscious voices (for his subject is always to some extent self-consciousness itself), the shapers of opinion in their own generation (or through delayed influence in the next), and must continually reassess their ringing assertions and denials. At any rate, in tracing the characteristic Victorian attitudes toward both public and private time, I have drawn largely upon the most eloquent of spokesmen—above all, the poets, and then the novelists and essayists—and especially those who did most to determine the temper of their own culture or have had the strongest impact upon ours. From such writers I have quoted very freely and often with little of my own commentary, for I have wished to let the Victorians speak for themselves of their common assumptions or, when there seemed to be no clear consensus, of the differences of feeling that lent a tension and vitality to the period. Yet quotations like statistics can of course be invoked to support any argument. The evidence I have here assembled is necessarily far from complete, for much of all that the Victorians wrote—and when articulate at all, they were usually voluminous—has relevance to our theme. My hope is merely that the illustrations in the following chapters may seem sufficiently numerous and cogent to represent Victorian literature as a whole and to suggest one of its abiding concerns.

Though this is a little book, my indebtedness in writing it has been large and cumulative. I am grateful to the John Simon Guggenheim Memorial Foundation for giving me the opportunity to read and think and travel in lands where time has many meanings. Parts of several chapters in somewhat different form served as lectures at Connecticut College, Boston College, the College of Wooster, and the University of Arizona, and I thank all of these institutions for providing sympathetic and critical captive audiences. Some sentences in my first chapter are drawn from a short paper which I read at the 1961 meeting of the Modern Language Association and which was later printed as "The Fourth Dimension of Victorianism" in the *Victorian Newsletter;* I appreciate the service of that journal in providing a wider forum for what was in effect the prospectus of this book. As always I owe much to the advice and good offices of my wife Elizabeth and to the help, direct and indirect, of many friends and colleagues, especially Howard Mumford Jones, Douglas Bush, Marjorie H. Nicolson, and Carl R. Woodring. Finally I inscribe this essay to Walter Jackson Bate, with whom over many years I have discussed many things —though scarcely my present subject, for, with him conversing, one forgets all time.

J. H. B.

Cambridge, Massachusetts
March 1966

CONTENTS

THE TRIUMPH OF TIME

THE FOUR FACES OF
VICTORIAN TIME

All the four faces of that Charioteer
Had their eyes banded . . .
                                        –Shelley

The Triumph of Life, the great dream-allegory that Shelley left unfinished at the time of his death, depicts the
whole human race led captive by the delusions of earthly
living. Through all history none have escaped, none "but
the sacred few . . . of Athens or Jerusalem," none, that is,
but Christ and Socrates. The vanquished, passing down a
broad highway, follow a triumphal car, ill-guided by a
four-faced charioteer with all eyes banded. The victor is
Life, and the charioteer is apparently Time, turned blindly
to all directions, past, present, future, and eternity.

To all modern men life and time seem inseparably linked,
and most are content to be led aimlessly through the drift
of experience. But the more sensitive ones demand some
perspective, a sense of time's course or meaning; like Shelley, who was pre-eminently one of them, they are forever
looking before and after, impatient with the mere flux of
things and eager to find a way once again of measuring
their brief lives under some eternal aspect.

It was in the nineteenth century, especially in Victorian
England, that many modern attitudes toward the whole
temporal process first emerged. The Victorians, at least as

1

their verse and prose reveal them, were preoccupied almost obsessively with time and all the devices that measure time's flight. The clock beats out the little lives of men in *In Memoriam*. Adam Bede in an anxious moment listens intently to a clock's "hard indifferent tick, . . . as if he had some reason for doing so." Hardy's clock-winder cancels out each sore sad day as he climbs nightly to "the trackway of Time" in an old church tower, where the clock itself wheezes rheumatically on. Hopkins's watch marches in step with the man, "Mortal my mate, bearing my rock-a-heart / Warm beat with cold beat company." The large watch that defines Mr. Dombey races with the doctor's watch across the silence as Mrs. Dombey lies dying. A chorus of bells and chimes striking the hour in a pawnshop makes time "instant and momentous" for Stevenson's Markheim. Rossetti's Blessed Damozel sees "Time like a pulse shake fierce / Through all the worlds," while the lovers in his *House of Life* cherish a silent noon when time is hushed and "still as the hour-glass." The egoists of Meredith's *Modern Love* have "fed not on the advancing hours," and over them, appropriately, "Time leers between, above his twiddling thumbs." Father Time behaves frighteningly as the son of Jude the Obscure. Time crawls "like a monstrous snake / Wounded and slow and very venomous" through the City of Dreadful Night. And the bird of Time flutters more relentlessly over FitzGerald's *Rubáiyát* than over Omar Khayyám's. Though sometimes stopped and sometimes accelerated, Time dominates even Wonderland, where the White Rabbit, consulting his pocket-watch, is constantly fearful lest he be late, and the mad tea-party lingers forever at six o'clock. "If you knew Time as well as I do," the Hatter tells Alice, "you wouldn't talk about wasting *it*. It's *him*."

Whatever the gender, time presents its several faces again and again throughout Victorian literature. Tennyson was concerned early and late with the relation of the temporal to the eternal; the Mystic of his first volume[1] hears "Time flowing in the middle of the night, / And all things creeping to a day of doom"; and the emperor Akbar, in his last, writes of the faithful who "Kneel adoring Him the Timeless in the flame that measures Time." Arnold made the attrition of private time the main subject of his poetry; and in his prose he sought constantly to evaluate the public present, the "modern element" in life and letters, in the light of the best that the past had thought and said, yet with an awareness also of "the natural and necessary stream of things"[2] leading to the future. Browning all his life strove both to recreate the dramatic past and to record the infinite moment. Swinburne on occasion yearned for a life beyond time, a life "that casts off time as a robe,"[3] but his most characteristic and perhaps his best poem remains the moving, rhapsodic "Triumph of Time," which hymns the irreversible passing of love.

More generous men than Scrooge were haunted by the ghosts of Past, Present, and Yet to Come. A new generation of historians, both literate and laborious, enlarged the limits of the human past and speculated on the possibility of finding patterns of recurrence or meaningful analogies with their own time. And almost every one of the major novelists attempted at least one historical novel, somehow relevant in theme to their own age, while many of the lesser ones peered into a more or less utopian future. The author of the standard biography frequently designed his work as a "Life and Times." The philosophic critic made a new appeal to a mysterious Time-spirit, the *Zeitgeist* determining the availability of modes and ideas. And the theologian, whether in the conservative *Tracts for the Times* or the liberal *Essays and Reviews,* asserted the role of the historic Church, the rites and dogmas evolving over long years, in the immediate life of the nineteenth century. Ruskin, who wrote "Time" in blank verse when he was only seven and *Praeterita,* his warm evocation of the personal past, when he was nearly seventy, paused in mid career—in his letters *Time and Tide*—to reflect that time and life were virtually one: " 'Time is money'; the words tingle in my ears so that I can't go on writing. Is it nothing better, then? If we could thoroughly understand that time was—*itself,*—would it not be more to the purpose? A thing of which loss or gain was absolute loss, and perfect gain."[4] Carlyle, on the other hand, whose interest in the problem is apparent not only in his histories but even in the titles of some of his other works, "Signs of the Times," *Past and Present, Latter-Day Pamphlets,* could recognize time as the great deluder. Speaking for all Carlyle's contemporaries, though in his own peculiar idiom, Teufelsdröckh complained: "Our whole terrestrial being is based on Time, and built of Time; it is wholly a Movement, a Time-impulse; Time is the author of it, the material of it . . . . O Time-Spirit, how hast thou environed and imprisoned us, and sunk us so deep in thy troublous dim Time-Element, that only in lucid moments can so much as glimpses of our upper Azure Home be revealed to us!"[5]

Man's concern with time had, of course, persisted since the beginning of time itself. It had engaged Zeno the Eleatic no less than Heraclitus of Ephesus. The death of time had fired the apocalyptic vision of St. John, and the ruins of time had provided a major theme to the Renaissance poets. On a far lower plane, men had long since learned to live by the clock; the Lilliputians had reason to believe that the god Gulliver worshiped was a watch, since he "called it his oracle, and said that it pointed out the time for every action of his life."

Nonetheless, as Carlyle suggested, nineteenth-century absorption in the troublous time-element differed both in kind and degree. The notion of public time, or history, as the medium of organic growth and fundamental change, rather than simply additive succession, was essentially new. Objects hitherto apparently stable had begun to lose their old solidity. Drawing on Lyell's geology, Tennyson saw in nature tangible evidence of a fluidity about which ancient philosophy had only speculated:

> The hills are shadows, and they flow
>   From form to form, and nothing stands;
>   They melt like mist, the solid lands,
> Like clouds they shape themselves and go.

The Victorians were entering a modern world, where, according to the angry Wyndham Lewis, "chairs and tables, mountains and stars, are animated into a magnetic restlessness, and exist on the same vital terms as man. They are as it were the lowest grade, the most sluggish of animals. All is alive; and, in that sense, all is mental."[6] When we so dissolve all things in time, said Lewis, we commit ourselves to cultural decadence, for true civilization has always depended on the classical virtues of permanence and order. Be that as it may, modern man is no more able to repudiate the time dimension than to reject the whole course of modern knowledge.

If the discovery of space has proceeded rapidly ever since the late Renaissance, the discovery of modern scientific time belongs largely to the past one hundred and fifty years, and the theory of relativity has made each dependent on the other. The object now has even less fixity than Tennyson imagined; it has become a range of charged energies in a space-time continuum. The "new sciences" of the nineteenth century—uniformitarian geology, nebular astronomy, evolutionary biology—were all sciences "in time," governed by temporal methodologies. The new physics, unlike its older mechanistic counterpart, acquired a time-direction with the second law of thermodynamics and the concept of entropy. And mathematics itself, the key to most scientific advance, turned to time, as it developed new theories of assemblages and continuous functions, theories which first adequately resolved Zeno's ancient paradox: how could the arrow in passage exist if it occupied no fixed point at any given moment of its flight? Meanwhile, the new social studies, emulating the more exact sciences, were all thoroughly grounded in the historical method.[7] Herbert Spencer with his great law of evolution, Karl Marx with his dialectical materialism, Sidney Webb with his faith in the inevitability of gradualism —to name only the three most conspicuous of the many social scientists living and working in Victorian England— each of these responded wholeheartedly to the dominion of public time as the age understood and defined its authority.

Toward the end of his long life Hardy pondered in awkward rhyme the irony of the "Fourth Dimension":

So, Time,
Royal, sublime,
Heretofore held to be
Master and enemy,
Thief of my Love's adornings,
Despoiling her to scornings:—
The sound philosopher
Now sets him to aver
You are nought
But a thought
Without reality.[8]

Though the theorists of relativity were heavily cerebral, this was not precisely the significance of the space-time continuum; for the scientists still dealt in an objective linear time to be measured quantitatively. The poet, on the other hand, was prepared to value only the far more complex private time, a qualitative force to be experienced, not to be measured, intense yet illusory, quite "without reality" apart from the psychological life of the individual. Many years before, Tennyson had allowed the erudite Princess Ida to explain the necessary subjectivity:

> For was, and is, and will be, are but is;
> And all creation is one act at once,
> The birth of light: but we that are not all,
> As parts, can see but parts, now this, now that,
> And live, perforce, from thought to thought, and make
> One act a phantom of succession: thus
> Our weakness somehow shapes the shadow, Time.

And the learned Master Whewell, once Tennyson's tutor at Cambridge, had apparently distinguished the subjective time from the objective when he announced that "time, like space, is not only a form of perception, but of *intuition*."[9]

So conceived, private time is arbitrary, relative in quality to the passing personal emotion, continuous, yet variable in tempo—now fast, now slow. Scott weighs "one crowded hour of glorious life" against "an age without a name"; and Byron's Manfred, in unequal argument with the unbyronic Chamois Hunter, who considers himself by far the older man, insists that life is to be reckoned by deeds, not years:

> Think'st thou existence doth depend on time?
> It doth; but actions are our epochs: mine
> Have made my days and nights imperishable,
> Endless, and all alike, as sands on the shore. . . .

In a quieter vein, Thackeray comments in *Esmond* that "at certain periods of life we live years of emotion in a few weeks—and look back on those times, as on great gaps between the old life and the new."[10] Stevenson tells the fable of a monk who, wandering in the woods, hears a bird sing just "a trill or two" and then, on his return, finds himself a stranger at the monastery gates; for he has been absent fifty years, so much has he been beguiled by "that time-devouring nightingale," romance.[11] Less fancifully, George Eliot in *The Mill on the Floss* describes how slowly time moves in the bedchamber of the stricken Mr. Tulliver as he shows signs of gradual recovery, and meanwhile how rapidly and efficiently the time outside consummates his financial ruin.

As seen by poet and novelist alike, human time thus defies scientific analysis and measurement; contracting and expanding at will, mingling before and after without ordered sequence, it pays little heed to ordinary logical relations. It is intelligible only as duration, as a constant indivisible flow in which life will be a continuous, enduring unity of change, and the consciousness, by memory and desire, will completely merge any given moment of the present with the whole personal past and future. Such a formulation, essentially Bergsonian, belongs largely to a post-Victorian period. But its terms were freely anticipated by various philosophies current in the nineteenth century, especially by those developing Hume's concept of the self as function rather than substance, a concept which made the psychological life an incessant movement in time. Walter Pater accordingly could argue in the most celebrated of his essays: "This at least of flame-like our life has, that it is but the concurrence, renewed from moment to moment, of forces parting sooner or later on their ways.

. . . Analysis . . . assures us that those impressions of the
individual mind to which, for each one of us, experience
dwindles down, are in perpetual flight. . . . It is with this
movement, with the passage and dissolution of impressions,
images, sensations, that analysis leaves off—that continual
vanishing away, that strange, perpetual weaving and un-
weaving of ourselves."[12]

Yet the endless movement was not limited to the insub-
stantial self. The Victorian, looking outwards, could see his
whole age in perpetual motion. And in this respect at least,
personal time was to a high degree consonant with public
time, with the actual objective history of the period. So
widespread and so rapid were the changes wrought by the
nineteenth century in the material conditions of living that
no one, however much he might wish to dwell in the spirit,
could altogether escape a sense of almost physical exhilara-
tion or bewilderment rushing in upon him. The hero of
"Locksley Hall" thrilled to the steamship and the railway as
to "thoughts that shake mankind." And there were to be
other and scarcely less impressive inventions: the telegraph,
the telephone, the sewing machine, the photograph, the gas
burner, the electric light, the typewriter, the automobile.
Increasingly rapid communication and transportation made
the farthest corners of the globe seem less and less remote.
The spread of the factory system virtually destroyed the
British agricultural economy and transformed the way of
life of toiling millions. The population multiplied at a stag-
gering rate, and London grew eight- or ten-fold within the
century, until it had become by far the world's largest and
most prosperous city.

"Take it all in all," wrote Frederic Harrison early in the
1880's, "the merely material, physical, mechanical change
in human life in the hundred years, from the days of Watt

and Arkwright to our own, is greater than occurred in the thousand years that preceded, perhaps even in the two thousand years or twenty thousand years."[13] Moreover, the speed of the change seemed to be constantly increasing. At the time of the Second Reform Bill, which widened the base of the franchise and so prepared the way for a broader democracy, Carlyle complained that his political fears were being realized with frightening rapidity: "the series of events comes swifter and swifter, at a strange rate; and hastens unexpectedly,—'velocity increasing' (if you will consider, for this too is as when the little stone has been loosened, which sets the whole mountain-side in motion) 'as the *square* of the time':—so that the wisest Prophecy finds it was quite wrong as to date; and, patiently, or even indolently waiting, is astonished to see itself fulfilled, not in centuries as anticipated, but in decades and years."[14] Carlyle's use of the ratio anticipated Henry Adams's "rule of phase," according to which each successive phase would last for the square root of the number of years in the preceding. And his dread of the acceleration foreshadowed the mood of Adams as he stood awe-struck at the Paris Exposition in 1900 before the great silent dynamo, the symbol to him of an incalculable "ultimate energy."[15]

In literature, however, and in the cultural life generally, the actual changes and the rate of their occurrence count for less than the emotional and intellectual responses, positive or negative, that they engender or that the very concept of change elicits. Though often opposed to particular innovations, many Victorians accepted the idea itself almost as an article of faith. If Carlyle came to resist a dreadful velocity, he was from the beginning convinced that progressive adaptation and sudden or gradual conversion, the constant rebirth of the spirit symbolized by the phoenix, were essential both to the individual man and to the whole society. For the latter, remarked Teufelsdröckh, "is not dead; that Carcass, which you call dead Society, is but her mortal coil which she has shuffled off, to assume a nobler; she herself, through perpetual metamorphoses, in fairer and fairer development, has to live till Time also merge in Eternity."[16] Ruskin, who deplored many modern developments, found Changefulness a central attribute of the creative achievement he most admired: "It is," he wrote, "that strange *disquietude* of the Gothic spirit that is its greatness; that restlessness of the dreaming mind, that wanders hither and thither among the niches, and flickers feverishly around the pinnacles, and frets and fades in labyrinthine knots and shadows along wall and roof, and yet is not satisfied, nor shall be satisfied. The Greek could stay in his triglyph furrow, and be at peace; but the work of the Gothic heart is fretwork still, and it can neither rest in, nor from, its labour, but must pass on, sleeplessly, until its love of change shall be pacified for ever in the change that must come alike on them that wake and them that sleep."[17] And Hopkins saw in all changeful, incandescent, dappled things a witness to the God "whose beauty is past change," and in the daily renewed freshness of nature a testimony that the Holy Ghost still broods over the whole bent world.

Other poets were less sanguine in their view of change, especially insofar as new modes and attitudes seemed to threaten the great traditions of art and society. Clough urged that the innovators "yet consider it again" before sweeping aside the legacy of two thousand years.[18] Tennyson as a young man declared "Raw Haste" to be "half-sister to Delay," and years later as Laureate he warned against the "fierce or careless looseners of the faith" and the new literary naturalists, dealers in "poisonous honey stolen from

France."[19] But it was Arnold above all who indicted his contemporaries for rushing precipitantly into action. "Let us think," he counseled, "of quietly enlarging our stock of true and fresh ideas, and not, as soon as we get an idea or half an idea, be running out with it into the street, and trying to make it rule there." Yet he had at no time much confidence that his advice would be heeded. In "The Scholar-Gypsy" he had diagnosed "this strange disease of modern life, / With its sick hurry," and bidden the legendary wanderer to remain immortal by escaping infection,

> For what wears out the life of mortal men?
>   'Tis that from change to change, their being rolls;
> 'Tis that repeated shocks, again, again,
>   Exhaust the energy of strongest souls
>   And numb the elastic powers.

Goethe, to be sure, he felt, had kept his luminous vitality in an age of violence and confusion, but only because his youth had been passed "in a tranquil world." The Victorians, on the other hand, he contended, had been conditioned from childhood to a general instability:

> . . . we brought forth and reared in hours
> of change, alarm, surprise—
> What shelter to grow ripe is ours?
> What leisure to grow wise?

Arnold was troubled by the vision of universal change governing all human affairs of past, present, and foreseeable future, and on occasion was even driven to imagine with dismay "Far regions of eternal change" beyond human experience altogether.[20]

The sense of history, of a perpetually changeful public time, was central to the intellectual life of the nineteenth century. But there were as many expressions on each of time's faces as there were thoughtful observers. "Each age," sang Arthur O'Shaughnessy, "is a dream that is dying, / Or one that is coming to birth";[21] and the assessment of rise or fall depended in large part on the predisposition of the dreamer. Whatever the historian's effort to achieve objectivity, public change could seldom for long be contemplated with a calm detachment; it called for evaluation as advance or decline, change for the better or change for the worse. The great polar ideas of the Victorian period were accordingly the idea of progress and the idea of decadence, the twin aspects of an all-encompassing history. Poised at their high moment in time, the Victorians, as we shall see, surveyed their world, its past and its future, with alternate hope and fear. Distant echoes of their positive faith and stronger reverberations of their misgiving reach down the years to our own age. We listen as to those who have already, like Stein in Conrad's *Lord Jim*, braved "the destructive element," which is time itself; and like Marlow, his auditor, we weigh the possibilities of our response: "The whisper of his conviction seemed to open before me a vast and uncertain expanse, as of a crepuscular horizon on a plain at dawn—or was it, perchance, at the coming of night? One had not the courage to decide. . . ."

❧ II ❧

THE USES OF HISTORY

How beautiful to see . . . , as through a long
vista, into the remote Time; to have, as it were, an
actual section of almost the earliest Past brought
safe into the Present, and set before your eyes!
  —Carlyle

Dɪᴄᴋ, the happy boatman of William Morris's
News from Nowhere, is too well contented with his own
time to have any real interest in the past, for, as his great-
grandfather has told him, "it is mostly in periods of turmoil
and strife and confusion that people care much about history."[1] Morris himself, however, despite all his euphoric
dreams of a distant bright tomorrow, "the wonderful days
a-coming," could never achieve such indifference; the child
of a quick uncertain century, he was always essentially
retrospective, nostalgic for the values of a lost culture.
What he once called his "passion for the history of the past
of mankind"[2] began in his boyhood, grew during his Oxford years and his association with the Pre-Raphaelites, and
remained strong even in the late utopian romance, where
the new life of Dick and his good companions derives
almost every attribute from an idealized medievalism.
Morris was the chief British influence on the modern movement in design. But whereas his great European contemporaries and the best of his English and American disciples

14

broke defiantly with the past in their search for new forms and their exploitation of new materials,[3] Morris spent his original talents and his almost boundless energy on a re-working of traditional motifs in time-honored media. His thought and practice alike relate him to an era more stren-uously devoted than any earlier one to the historical record and the historical method.

Though the society of Nowhere is brought into being by violence, most Victorians, including Morris himself in his less belligerent moods, preferred to think that reform might be achieved by the due processes of natural growth. Evolu-tion rather than revolution seemed the true way of history. Revolution, the upsetting of a fixed order, presupposed a clash of stable entities and essentially a static view of human nature; by the law of the eternal return, the spin of for-tune's wheel, the same forces would continually recur. Evolution, on the other hand, meant an organic growth of all things in time, a development in which the past, though never repeating itself, would persist through each successive modification. The past accordingly became the object of solicitous regard; the present could not be cut off from its history; civilization was a branching plant which would droop and wither if its roots were neglected or dislodged. The organic image, applied both to nature and to human culture, replaced the standard eighteenth-century mechan-istic analogy; the world was no longer a machine operating on a set cycle, but a living body fulfilling itself in constant adaptation to new conditions. As a skeptical rationalist John Morley had little respect for the theology of the Ox-ford Movement; yet he felt obliged in all honesty to com-mend the Tractarians for drawing attention "to history and the organic connection between past and present."[4] Ruskin felt that great architecture, mellowing with the years, served a familiar function as a vital link with the past; the noble building, he said, "connects forgotten and following ages with each other, and half constitutes the identity, as it concentrates the sympathy, of nations; it is in that golden stain of time, that we are to look for the real light, and colour, and preciousness of architecture."[5] The sense of history thus engendered a notion of the meaningful continuity of human experience.

But if the past was relevant to the life of the present, it was nonetheless no simple foreshadowing. It had its own complex integrity and was to be understood, if at all, only on its own terms. Anachronism was no longer acceptable. The Italian masters had painted Biblical subjects arrayed in Florentine drapery against a Tuscan landscape, and Shakespeare had given his Romans and Plantagenets Elizabethan idiom and manners; but Victorian historical painters and novelists undertook much conscientious research in order to reproduce the past with a literal and, in effect, often quite pedantic accuracy. History could provide relevant standards of measurement, of comparison or contrast with the nineteenth century. Or sometimes it might be made to stand in mocking aloofness, like the ancient relics in the backgrounds of Hardy's Wessex, survivals of a bolder and more purposeful age. "Shall the Parthenon be in ruins on its rock," Ruskin asked the mill-owners of Bradford, "and Bolton priory in its meadow, but these mills of yours be the consummation of the buildings of the earth, and their wheels be as the wheels of eternity?"[6] But to whatever use the past might be put, each historical reference was expected to rest upon a studious regard for fact and an ability to enter, at least for the moment, imaginatively, even empathically, into the life of another society.

"The world," Morris insisted, "has been noteworthy for more than one century and one place, a fact which we are

pretty much apt to forget."⁷ The Victorians, however, despite the self-complacency of which they liked to accuse
each other, scarcely needed to be so reminded, for they
were steadily extending the limits of time and space.
Whereas the Georgian historians had been principally concerned with classical Greece and Rome and the nearly
contemporary English past, the Victorians discovered many
other areas of interest and significance. Perhaps most conspicuous was the close study of the medieval period, to
which the Romantic poets and Gothic novelists had already
prepared a sympathetic response. Especially with the founding of the Camden Society in 1838, devoted to the recovery
and examination of manuscripts, new light began to break
from the dark ages.⁸ But attention was also turned to Hebrew history and to Egyptian and Russian and East Asian,
to the English Renaissance and the Byzantine empire, to the
French Revolution and the colonial period in America.

As the widened view of the past carried over to literature, Browning, for example, could set his monologues with
assurance against more or less precisely dated Italian or
Spanish or French or Palestinian backgrounds. Tennyson
could look for subject matter not only to Greek mythology,
which provided some of his happiest inspirations, but also
to Anglo-Saxon times as in *Harold* and "The Battle of
Brunanburh," to Tudor history as in *Queen Mary*, to
medieval romance as in *Idylls of the King*, to records of
Akbar of Hindustan, to accounts of Lao-tse and Christopher Columbus and the Hawaiian heroine Kapiolani. And
Arnold, though the foremost apologist for the classical tradition, could derive his best known narratives from quite
unclassical sources, summaries—in travel books, histories,
and literary journals—of the ancient Persian tale of Rustum,
the Scandinavian myth of Balder, and the medieval legends
of Tristram and Saint Brandan.⁹

From the monumental work of George Grote to that of
J. B. Bury much distinguished Victorian scholarship was
devoted to the history of Greece; yet it became increasingly
clear that the Greeks themselves, especially when measured
against the time-conscious Hebrews, were deficient in a
true sense of history. The Greeks, complained Macaulay,
had no real notion of change and progress; they were ex-
clusive and self-sufficient, contemptuous of what the outside world might contribute to the further development of
their culture: "We cannot call to mind a single expression
of any Greek writer earlier than the age of Augustus, in-
dicating an opinion that anything worth reading could be
written in any language except his own."[10] The moderns
were therefore, according to Macaulay, far superior to the
ancients in the philosophy of history, and the difference
was "a difference not in degree but of kind." The moderns
apparently assumed an organic rather than a static society,
and they could no longer be so parochial as to believe that
the noteworthy belonged merely to one century and one
place.

    With so wide-ranging an interest in the past, the Victo-
rian period was inevitably a great age of revivals—the
Greek, the Gothic, the Renaissance, the Georgian—some of
which reached unexpected extremes. The Hellenism of
Arnold was perhaps a reasonable deduction from the study
of Greek culture; that of Swinburne, though without doubt
more erudite, was highly idiosyncratic and in effect sub-
versive of all rational order. Ruskin, who revered the true
nature of Gothic, deplored his own influence in helping
spread sham-Gothic towers and villas across the darkened
landscape. W. E. Henley, who joined enthusiastically in
the revaluation of eighteenth-century literature, assailed the
antiquarians responsible for "the canonisation (in figures)

of Chippendale and Sheraton."[11] The rebirth of the Renaissance led Browning to cherish the vigor and diversity of the quattrocento and Walter Pater to conclude that all the old masters had in some way anticipated a Paterian malaise. And the medieval revival prompted both the stringent ironies of Carlyle's *Past and Present* and the athletic absurdities of the Eglinton Tournament, the self-conscious simplicity of the Pre-Raphaelite ballads and the contrived ornateness of the Kelmscott Chaucer. Motifs from various past cultures were often brought into odd uneasy combination. Eclecticism, common throughout the period, was probably most conspicuous in the Aesthetic Movement and most amusingly caricatured in Gilbert's *Patience*. Bunthorne of the operetta, clearly a "Francesca da Rimini, niminy, piminy" young man, confesses that his medievalism's affectation and proceeds to sing of the palmy days of Queen Anne and the modish court of Empress Josephine; and Lady Jane speculates on a likely new uniform for the Dragoons: "There *is* a cobwebby grey velvet, with a tender bloom like cold gravy, which, made Florentine fourteenth-century, trimmed with Venetian leather and Spanish altar lace, and surmounted with something Japanese—it matters not what—would at least be Early English!" Many of the revivalists were hardly less exuberant in raiding the past, though most were rather more precise in their use of terms.

Since to understand is usually in some degree to condone, the deepening knowledge of other times and places engendered an increased relativity of judgment. Alarmed at the new readiness of moral compromise (specifically at the Victorian will to rationalize the political crimes of Louis Napoleon in order to live at peace with the Second Empire), Morley pointed to "the growth of the Historic Method" as the most important intellectual cause of the dominant mode of thought and sentiment. This method, as he defined it, involved "the comparison of the forms of an idea, or a usage, or a belief, at any given time, with the earlier forms from which they were evolved, or the later forms into which they were developed, and the establishment, from such a comparison, of an ascending and descending order among the facts." It consisted "in the explanation of existing parts in the frame of society by connecting them with corresponding parts in some earlier frame; in the identification of present forms in the past, and past forms in the present." Concern with origins, with the etiology of things, was, he said, the chief characteristic of nineteenth-century science, and it carried over to the whole moral and intellectual life of the time. Once men asked whether an idea was true, whether a policy was sound and good; now they asked how the idea came to be credited, how the policy was adopted and developed. Morley feared that, if carried too far, the Historic Method might "make men shrink from importing anything like absolute quality into their propositions" and lead them to regard strength of conviction and the resolute pursuit of good "as equivocal virtues of very doubtful perfection, in a state of things where every abuse has after all had a defensible origin."[12] Yet he himself was too firmly committed to the uses of history to believe that the method, if "rightly limited," would sanction such conclusions; he was determined that his own comparisons of past and present should inhibit neither his value-judgments nor his reforming zeal.

Meanwhile, historical relativism, scarcely limited at all, was making its most conspicuous assault on the absolutes of

religious fundamentalism. Subjecting the Bible to the same
sort of analysis brought to bear upon any other ancient
documents, the Higher Critics, at first in Germany but
from the early nineteenth century also in England, raised
problems of provenance, dating, authorship, stylistic consistency, and analogues in non-Hebraic literature—in short,
questioned the reliability of the scriptural canon and the
extent to which it might be regarded as inspired revelation.
Though more recent masters of the Higher Criticism have
frequently worked within the framework of Christian
orthodoxy, the early practitioners were for the most part
secular in effect and often also in intention. Perhaps the
most influential of these, though not the most scholarly,
D. F. Strauss was somewhat less bleakly rationalistic than
his colleagues at Tübingen, insofar as he granted that the
gospel story, though without historical validity, might have
a mythic significance. Yet his speculations were hardly reassuring to young Victorians whose faith was being under-
mined by his corrosive analysis. George Eliot translated his
Leben Jesu in 1846 with an unbroken grim determination,
often thoroughly "Strauss-sick" of soul.[13] And Clough,
whose "Epi-Strauss-ium" attempted a reassertion of value,
recorded his deeper distress and confusion in "Easter Day,
Naples, 1849." Browning, on the other hand, convinced
that Strauss's mythmongering was vacuous, satirized the
logic of a very Strauss-like German lecturer:

> So, he proposed inquiring first
> Into the various sources whence
>   This Myth of Christ is derivable;
> Demanding from the evidence,
>   (Since plainly no such life was livable)
> How these phenomena should class?
> Whether 'twere best opine Christ was,

Or never was at all, or whether
He was and was not, both together—
It matters little for the name,
So the idea be left the same.
Only for practical purpose' sake,
'Twas obviously as well to take
The popular story,—understanding
    How the ineptitude of the time,
And the penman's prejudice, expanding
    Fact into fable fit for the clime,
Had by slow and sure degrees, translated it
    Into this myth, this individuum—
Which, when reason had strained and abated it
    Of foreign matter, left, for residuum,
A Man!—a right true man, however,
Whose work was worthy a man's endeavour.[14]

Yet Browning's parody, though it struck brilliantly at
the misapplied historical method and the half-hearted will
to restore with one hand what the other had taken away,
could do little to check the efforts of Biblical critics as
solemn as Strauss and far less erudite. Fifteen years after
the poem J. R. Seeley, with no real knowledge of either
history or theology, issued his own life of Jesus, the anon-
ymous *Ecce Homo*, in the bland conviction that he could
place himself "in imagination at the time when he whom
we call Christ bore no such name" and then proceed "to
trace his biography from point to point, and accept those
conclusions about him, not which church doctors or even
apostles have sealed with their authority, but which the
facts themselves, critically weighed, appear to warrant."[15]
Seeley sought to affirm a Christian ethic purged of Christian dogma, but his attempt, like all others, to read the Bible
in terms of human history robbed religion of its nonhis-
torical dimension. The appeal to time denied the sanction
of eternity.

But the new sense of history was not necessarily so disruptive to religious conviction. Many saw the Incarnation as the central event of public time, the temporal life of Jesus which gave a meaning and direction from beyond history to the whole historical process; and Hopkins spoke eloquently for all these when he dated the "instress" of Christ that "rides time like riding a river": "It dates from day / Of his going in Galilee."[16] Mark Pattison, in the best of the pieces contributed to *Essays and Reviews,* insisted on an informed historical approach to Anglicanism, since "both the Church and the world of to-day are what they are as the result of the whole of their antecedents."[17] Newman, however, sharing something of the same historical bias, came to repudiate the whole Anglican position. "Whatever history teaches," he wrote, "whatever it omits, whatever it exaggerates or extenuates, whatever it says and unsays, at least the Christianity of history is not Protestantism. . . . To be deep in history is to cease to be a Protestant."[18]

And Newman himself was so deep in the subject that his conversion to Roman Catholicism has been called "an experience in history."[19] His *Essay on the Development of Christian Doctrine,* written in large part to explain the course of his *own* development, accounted for the presence of later Roman dogmas (which as an Anglican he had attacked) by a theory of evolutionary growth: ideas at first merely implicit and undetected had been articulated and clarified over the ages, and new interpretations had been adopted to meet the needs not of a static institution but of an organic body growing steadily in time. On its appearance in 1845 the book not only helped set a precedent of apologetic method in theology, but also more generally, according to Lord Acton, did much to make Englishmen "think historically, and watch the process as well as the result."[20] Yet Newman was concerned from the outset that the secular discipline of history should be properly checked so as to make no encroachments on the ultimate verities. "The evidence of History," he said, "is invaluable in its place; but, if it assumes to be the sole means of gaining Religious Truth, it goes beyond its place."[21] He thus for a while encouraged the free researches of Acton and Richard Simpson as Liberal Catholic historians, but he quickly withdrew his support as soon as he suspected that their liberalism was going too far in the exposure of past expediency and mismanagement within the church hierarchy. He feared that the unnecessary publication of unpleasant facts could serve only to weaken common regard for the cause that commanded his total allegiance. Until the end his own keen historical sense was governed by forces more compelling and decisive than itself: his will to believe and his capacity for faith.

Newman's respect for the long traditions of a church which had fostered "the religious life of millions upon millions of Christians for nearly twenty centuries,"[22] contrasts sharply with John Stuart Mill's contention that neither in religion nor in any other area of thought was a consensus of past opinion a sound index of truth. And the difference in emphasis almost marks a difference in generations. Newman's historical perspective aligned him with the most characteristic thinkers and writers of the Victorian period. Mill's relative indifference to history, at least as consecration in time, links him (though he was actually the younger man) to an earlier age. Despite his discovery of Coleridge as a corrective of Bentham, Mill was—no less than the lat-

ter—opposed to the organic theory of the state. "Human
beings in society," he wrote, "have no properties but those
which are derived from, and may be resolved into, the laws
of the nature of individual man."[23] He failed to see that the
individual might be subject to varying pressures with
changing social conditions or that the group at any moment might be greater than the sum of its parts. And,
though he valued individuality, he assumed a certain uni-
formity from age to age in the motives and responses of
human beings. He was thus able in his *Principles of Political
Economy* to conceive of "Economic Man" as a fixed entity,
and quite unable to understand the logic of Ruskin's *Unto
This Last* attacking that concept. Mill's most enduring
book, the great essay *On Liberty*, appeared in 1859, the
year of *The Origin of Species*, but his thought was essentially pre-Darwinian in its premises, that is to say, virtually
untouched by the evolutionary idea (which had of course
been current in various forms long before Darwin's book).
Herbert Spencer, though far less ready to advocate social
reform, was a more advanced political theorist insofar as he
postulated a society, forever evolving, articulating its will
in a continuous progressive development. Nor did the
Fabians, however high their regard for Mill's mind and
work, underestimate the notion of historical process opera-
tive in a social organism. As their name suggests, they were
resigned to the necessity of gradual change to be effected
through a patient, though zealous, political education; they
strove to replace "deductive Economics" with "inductive
Sociology,"[24] generalities about hypostatized Economic
Man with specific studies of real men in their own place
and time.

The new "inductive Sociology" was patently influenced

by the approach of Victorian science. At the very beginning of the period (actually within a month of the Queen's
accession) Macaulay's essay on Bacon offered a vigorous
apology for the one method that was to dominate nineteenth-century research, the inductive method to which
Bacon had first given "importance and dignity." The description of the wonders of Solomon's House in *The New
Atlantis,* said Macaulay, owed nothing to any fancies "beyond the mighty magic of induction and of time." And the
two—induction and time—clearly belonged together; for
science admitted no sudden inference, no "scanty and hasty
induction" such as would have satisfied the older philosophers; it demanded laborious "experiment after experiment," careful reasoning from more and more data. This
was the true inductive method, and "the only method . . .
by which new truth can be discovered."[25] Years later T. H.
Huxley, the most responsible publicist of Darwinism,
agreed. Baconian induction was the only way to learn the
causes of things—"the method of scientific investigation
being the same for all orders of facts and phenomena what-
soever."[26] None of the Victorians could foresee the extent
to which twentieth-century science with its firmer rooting
in mathematical theory would become conceptual rather
than simply empirical, deductive rather than merely inductive. But a good many responded to the claims of induction;
fresh and free inquiry seemed a necessary corrective of
such old postulates as new facts no longer supported.

Geology was the first of the "new" sciences to strike the
Victorian imagination with disturbing impact. As long ago
as 1785 James Hutton had argued that geological change
must have occurred by regular processes over an immeas-
urably long time. But the orthodox theory of the earth,

through the eighteen thirties and even into the forties, remained catastrophism, the notion that sudden cataclysms
of nature, violent upheavals and inundations, had given the
world its shape and structure. The catastrophic theory was
tenaciously held by the fundamentalists insofar as it seemed
in accord with the Mosaic account of creation and the relatively brief chronology of Bishop Ussher, who had traced
the beginning of things to 4004 B.C.; indeed it was more
clearly a deduction from the Bible record than the product
of scientific observation. Charles Lyell's *Principles of Geology*, however, presented the contrary and modern view of
geological time. Working from inductive studies of present
processes, Lyell developed at due length the theory of uni-
formitarianism, the doctrine, that is, of slow change
wrought by such quiet agents as erosion and sedimentary
deposit, forces everywhere still evident; his book, as its
subtitle suggests, was "an attempt to explain the former
changes of the Earth's surface by reference to causes now
in action." "We are prepared," he wrote, "to find that in
time also, the confines of the universe lie beyond the reach
of mortal ken. But in whatever direction we pursue our
researches, whether in time or space, we discover everywhere the clear proofs of a Creative Intelligence, and of
His foresight, wisdom, and power."[27] Yet the new vision
was scarcely reassuring to those who had learned to think
in terms of a more human, more manageable time-scheme.
The catastrophists continued to resist for some years after
1833 when the third and last volume of the *Principles* appeared, and the fundamentalists considered the whole theory a flagrant blasphemy. Tennyson, on the other hand,
who was very early in his reading and acceptance of Lyell,
meditated on the terrible vastness of a geological time

mocking every short moment of man's effort and affection:

> Might I not say, "Yet even here,
>   But for one hour, O Love, I strive
>   To keep so sweet a thing alive"?
> But I should turn mine ears and hear
>
> The moanings of the homeless sea,
>   The sound of streams that swift or slow
>   Draw down Aeonian hills, and sow
> The dust of continents to be;
>
> And Love would answer with a sigh,
>   "The sound of that forgetful shore
>   Will change my sweetness more and more,
> Half-dead to know that I shall die."[28]

And Ruskin, more reluctantly receiving specific new evidences, could feel the geologists hammering at the bedrock of his own belief: "If only," he complained, "the Geologists would let me alone, I could do very well, but those dreadful Hammers. I hear the clink of them at the end of every cadence of the Bible verses."[29]

But even if the evolution of nature required a much longer period than Bishop Ussher had calculated, it was not immediately clear that men had inhabited the earth for more than the six allotted millennia. Not until the eighteen fifties when Lyell's theory had at last established its supremacy did the archaeologists, who drew heavily on his work, succeed in demonstrating conclusively the greater antiquity of man.[30] Then, almost simultaneously, William Pengelly at Brixham in Devonshire and Joseph Prestwich and John Evans at the Somme uncovered tools buried beside the remains of long extinct animals. It was now quite certain, Evans told the Society of Antiquaries in June 1859, "that in a period of antiquity remote beyond any of which we have hitherto found traces, this portion of the globe was peopled by man."[31] So began the concept of prehistory, according to which the length of human existence on earth would eventually be reckoned as some six hundred thousand, rather than merely six thousand, years. Sir John Lubbock's *Prehistoric Times*, published in 1865, introduced the terms Paleolothic and Neolithic to designate two successive Stone Ages greatly antedating all written records. Later Victorian archaeologists, in particular the appropriately named General Pitt-Rivers and Flinders Petrie, brought increased assurance and precision to the examination of sites and the analysis of all available evidence. The frontiers of history, or prehistory, were pushed farther and farther back, and the perspectives of human time widened enormously. Meanwhile, Darwinian biology was pointing in the same direction. Man, like all other animals, had evolved—and was evolving—in a long slow time now to be subdivided and named and classified. In the nineteenth century the natural scientist moved closer than ever before to the approach and concern of the historian.

And the historian learned in many ways to emulate the scientists. History became an inductive discipline, an empirical study devoted to the amassing of facts without preconceived theory or metaphysical assumption. In Germany the great Ranke declared it his purpose neither to instruct nor to moralize but to present the past as it had really been; and the British "scientific" historians under his influence, especially Lord Acton and later J. B. Bury, fully shared his aspiration.[32] Froude complained that history was not properly so "scientific" as it appeared to be in the work of

H. T. Buckle, who believed that all human affairs were
"reducible to laws, and could be made as intelligible as the
growth of the chalk cliffs or the coal measures." The historian, said Froude, must grant that new movements in
human progress are subject to the almost infinite variety of
human interests and emotions and accordingly are far less
predictable than events charted by the natural sciences; yet
he could—and should—strive to approximate a scientific
objectivity. According to Froude, the best history contained the least speculation and the most eloquent facts:
"the thought about the thing must change as we change;
but the thing itself can never change." Ideally history
should be written like drama: "Wherever possible, let us
not be told *about* this man or that. Let us hear the man
himself speak; let us see him act, and let us be left to form
our own opinions about him."[33] In other words, the historian must achieve the empathy that Herder long before
had demanded of him;[34] he must feel the totality of the past
and then proceed to recreate it as a living entity in the
present; above all, he must remove himself, his own hopes
and fears and judgments, from his research and writing.
And his history would then be as inscrutable as a work of
art, where the meanings are only implicit and the moral, if
any, cannot be abstracted from its vehicle.

Many of the "scientific" historians would have rejected
Froude's aesthetic analogy; for the dramatist clearly, even
though objectively, shapes his materials to suit his design,
and the scientist is less free to ignore or exclude incon-
venient data. But all accepted the principle of detachment,
and all were so deeply committed to a phenomenological
view that they felt little inclination in any case to general-
ize or to discover large patterns of significance or consis-

tency. Ultimately, overwhelmed by concrete particulars, most abdicated altogether the responsibility of evaluating the long complex process of human time. And a new generation of "historicists," well schooled in the science, learned to deny that there was any meaning to assess.

Nevertheless, despite his preference for the objectivity of drama, Froude conceded that "philosophies of history, sciences of history—all these, there will continue to be; the fashions of them will change, as our habits of thought will change; each new philosopher will find his chief employment in showing that before him no one understood anything." The nineteenth century was in fact the golden age of the ideologists, intent on discovering or inventing patterns of growth and decay. And however insistently later historians may affirm the dogma of meaninglessness,[35] which is itself merely another hypothesis, the search for purpose and coherence persists even into our own time; it seems a necessary expression of man's never quite forgotten need to believe that the human enterprise may be more than a great delusion. Philosophies of history may seem patently subjective; but, if all history is, as R. G. Collingwood suggested, a re-enactment of the past in the mind of the historian, then objectivity itself is a highly relative achievement.

Traditionally, Hebrew and Christian thought alike assumed that history under God's guidance was moving inevitably toward its goal either in time or eternity and that the final dispensation would make intelligible all the anomalies of the process. This providential view, of course, frequently recurs in the Victorian period. Most conspicuously perhaps, it provides the resolution of *In Memoriam*, where a recovered faith in love and life itself is recognized as "comrade of the lesser faith / That sees the course of human things"; there have, the poet concedes, certainly been defeats and betrayals, and "No doubt vast eddies in the flood / Of onward time shall yet be made," but the man of faith can now

> see in part
> That all, as in some piece of art,
> Is toil coöperant to an end,

and be confident accordingly that the whole creation moves to "one far-off divine event."

But there were also current more secular attitudes, which bore traces of various new philosophies. Kant had regarded history as the process by which mankind was becoming rational. Hegel had seen in it not the fulfillment of a predetermined and superimposed plan but the action and reaction of inherent forces, the relentless dialectic of change. Marx, working from Hegelian premises, developed his concept of a dialectical materialism leading to the socialist state. Comte meanwhile had defined the three stages of civilization: the theological phase superseded by the metaphysical and that in turn replaced by the scientific or positive. And Herbert Spencer announced the great ground-rule of evolution, the movement of all things in time from "an indefinite, incoherent homogeneity" to "a definite coherent heterogeneity." All these postulated the progress of history, and all, whether or not they were aware of the fact, presupposed some immanent will dictating the progressive direction. Similarly, on a more practical level, Macaulay took for granted a constant historical advance, whatever its action might be. And Winwood Reade, author of the popular *Martyrdom of Man*, argued —somewhat illogically for a convinced rationalist—that "in each generation the human race has been tortured that their children might profit by their woes."[36]

Throughout the century the idea of progress had to contend with less sanguine cyclic theories of cultural growth, decay, death, and rebirth, and the pessimistic concept of decadence. But to the modern historian these notions likewise may seem unwarranted assumptions. Collingwood, at any rate, insisted that "in history . . . there are no mere phenomena of decay: every decline is also a rise, and it is only the historian's personal failures of knowledge or sympathy . . . that prevent him from seeing this double character, at once creative and destructive, of any historical process whatever."[37]

Among the Victorians, Ruskin apparently sensed the danger of making a partial estimate, for he warned students of history that "all evidences of progress or decline have . . . to be collected in mass,—then analyzed with extreme care—then weighed in the balance of the Ages, before we can judge the meaning of any one."[38] Yet he himself was seldom so cautious; he made bold, rapid intuitive judgments of the health or sickness of whole cultural epochs. In the meanings of the past he sought and found clues to the significance of his own confused society and perhaps of life itself. Like Morris he was conscious of living at a time when he could not but "care much about history," and like most of his contemporaries he expressed his concern with a strong emotional commitment.

❦ III ❧

THE IDEA OF PROGRESS

Not in vain the distance beacons. Forward,
    forward let us range,
Let the great world spin forever down the ringing
    grooves of change.

Through the shadow of the globe we sweep into
    the younger day;
Better fifty years of Europe than a cycle of Cathay.
                                                    –Tennyson

"WE ARE on the side of progress," wrote Macaulay early in his career, assured even then that his editorial plural might resound as the voice of a new generation. "From the great advances which European society has made, during the last four centuries, in every species of knowledge, we infer, not that there is no room for improvement, but that, in every science which deserves the name, immense improvements may be confidently expected." "The history of England," he continued, "is emphatically the history of progress. It is the history of a constant movement of the public mind, of a constant change in the institutions of a great society"—and, of course, of general change for the better. "To us, we will own, nothing is so interesting and delightful as to contemplate the steps by which the England of Domesday Book, the England of the Curfew and the Forest Laws, the England of the crusaders, monks,

34

schoolmen, astrologers, serfs, outlaws, became the England which we know and love, the classic ground of liberty and philosophy, the school of all knowledge, the mart of all trade."[1] "We rely," he said elsewhere, "on the natural tendency of the human intellect to truth, and on the natural tendency of society to improvement. . . . History is full of the signs of this natural progress of society."[2]

The sanction for all such progress lay in the inductive method, which, as we have seen, Macaulay advocated with every resource of exuberant overstatement. The old philosophy asking unanswerable questions about fate and evil and the quality of happiness "could not be progressive"; but the new Baconian thought, centered on utility, made certain the "great and constant progress" of mankind:

It has lengthened life; it has mitigated pain; it has extinguished diseases; . . . it has extended the range of the human vision; it has multiplied the power of the human muscles; it has accelerated motion; it has annihilated distance; it has facilitated intercourse, correspondence, all friendly offices, all despatch of business; it has enabled man to descend to the depths of the sea, to soar into the air, to penetrate securely into the noxious recesses of the earth, to traverse the land in cars which whirl along without horses, and the ocean in ships which run ten knots an hour against the wind. These are but a part of its fruits, and of its first fruits. For it is a philosophy which never rests, which has never attained, which is never perfect. Its law is progress.[3]

Prince Albert saw a ready instance of the "law" at work in the Great Exhibition of 1851, which, he believed, would help accomplish "that great end to which indeed all history points, the realisation of the unity of mankind."[4] The hero of Tennyson's "Locksley Hall" would surely have shared the prince's optimism, though, like Macaulay, he preferred to believe that the goal of progress, far from being im-

mediately attainable, was itself progressive, moving and
enlarging as fast as it was approached:

> Yet I doubt not through the ages one increasing
>   purpose runs,
> And the thoughts of man are widened with the process
>   of the suns.

The far future would accordingly have marvels in store
beyond even the present miracles of steam and rail:

> For I dipt into the future, far as human eye
>   could see,
> Saw the vision of the world, and all the wonder
>   that would be.

In such a sanguine mood the early Victorians gave the
very word "future" a new connotation; the future was a
better and brighter time to come.[5] Yet the future would
be "better" only insofar as the present was already good;
it would be but an extension of present improvements on
the past. By the time of the Exhibition faith in a Ma-
caulayan progress had engendered a confident complacency, which was to persist in some quarters, though more
and more seriously challenged to the end of the century
and even beyond. Late in the period William Morris rightly
identified the principal opposition to his Socialist program
as "the *Whig* frame of mind, natural to the modern prosperous middle-class men, who, in fact, so far as mechanical
progress is concerned, have nothing to ask for, if only
Socialism would leave them alone to enjoy their plentiful
style."[6] Macaulay could scarcely have understood Morris's
objection to so commonsensical an attitude.

And there was of course an unprecedented mechanical
progress throughout the Victorian era. Two recent his-

tories of technology, one in definitive detail, devote nearly as much space to the nineteenth century as to all other past centuries combined,[7] and in view of the evidence they assemble, it is difficult to imagine how men actually lived in the relatively unmechanized ages before the Industrial Revolution. The innovations that delighted Macaulay and the young man of "Locksley Hall" were little more than by-products of a general scientific advance. Whole new areas were discovered and explored: the worlds of infra-red and ultra-violet, electrodes and ions, electro-magnetism, thermodynamics, organic chemistry, vector analysis in the new mathematics, spectrum analysis in the new astrophysics. So firm was the assumption of progress, on the simplest material level, that many of the new devices and contrivances were destroyed as soon as superseded, with the result that historians now have inadequate records of the full range of mechanical invention during a period which in most other respects is amply documented.[8] Yet artifacts enough remain to suggest that the ingenuity was considerable.

Nor was the progress merely mechanical. The Victorians succeeded remarkably both in meeting the social challenge of industrialism and in widening the base of democracy. Despite the new horrors of the factory system, which were gradually mitigated or removed by legislation, most workers were better fed, clothed, and housed than their ancestors had been, and the improvement whetted their desire for further reform.[9] After the agitation and unrest of the thirties and forties, Victorian England enjoyed a new sense of order and security and, at least from the Great Exhibition of 1851 to the great depression of 1873, an almost unbroken prosperity. Notable advances were made in sanitation, town planning, public instruction.

Religious toleration and liberty steadily increased. Old legal codes were sharply revised and updated. The rights of the individual were guaranteed by law more surely than ever before.

At a time when many of these changes were still remote, Dickens, writing a new preface to *Pickwick,* found it "curious and interesting . . . to mark what important social improvements" had already taken place in the eleven short years since the novel's first appearance. "Legal reforms," he conceded, "have pared the claws of Messrs. Dodson and Fogg; a spirit of self-respect, mutual forbearance, education, and co-operation, for such good ends, has diffused itself among their clerks; places far apart are brought together, to the present convenience and advantage of the Public . . .: the laws relating to the imprisonment for debt are altered; and the Fleet Prison is pulled down." Possibly by the end of the century, he speculated, it might be discovered "that the universal diffusion of common means of decency and health is as much the right of the poorest of the poor, as it is indispensable to the safety of the rich, and of the State."[10] But there was less expectation than moral outrage in Dickens's forward glance, and already a hint of his darkening vision of society. A more sanguine observer would have seen behind the present improvements the law of progress which would assure an inevitable and unlimited advance in the future.

The idea of progress, however, as Macaulay and most of the early Victorians accepted it, had not always been a common assumption. It was virtually unknown in classical Greece and Rome[11] and generally alien to the spirit of medieval Europe; and it played no great part in the Renaissance, when men were concerned less with future prospects than with the humanistic past and the fullness of their own creative energies. It can be associated with the confident expectations of the Royal Society in Restoration England. But it made its first decisive appearance in France, late in the reign of Louis XIV, as an issue in the Quarrel of the Ancients and the Moderns, which followed Charles Perrault's eulogy of the culture of his own time as in many respects superior to the glories of Augustan Rome. Extending the argument from literature to the intellectual life on all levels, Fontenelle insisted that, since human nature was forever constant, the moderns could repeat past successes and add new triumphs of their own. Before long the way was open for the bolder assertions of the eighteenth-century rationalists and reformers, the philosophes and the physiocrats. Once progress was admitted as a possibility, it became a necessity, a "law" governing present and future. To the Abbé de Saint-Pierre man's destiny was a perpetual social advance. Helvétius believed that human character could be indefinitely molded by progressive laws and institutions. Turgot declared that "the total mass of the human race marches continually though sometimes slowly towards an ever-increasing perfection."[12] And Condorcet went to the guillotine with the unshaken conviction that the study of history firmly established the idea of Progress and helped man determine the direction of future reform and accelerate its course. "The idea of progress, . . ." said Guizot some years later, "seems to me the fundamental idea contained in the word *civilisation*."[13]

Eighteenth-century England was somewhat slower than France to receive the notion with approval. Swift, whose *Battle of the Books* continued the Quarrel of the Ancients and the Moderns, was clearly on the side of the Ancients and all his life suspicious of progressive "projectors" both in science and in government. And Mandeville in his *Fable of the Bees* set out to prove that private vices were so deeply ingrained in men as to preclude any general moral progress. In the latter part of the century, however, the idea found vigorous support, particularly among the rationalists and radicals. Joseph Priestley believed an indefinite progress possible since man's reason was infinite. Adam Smith saw progress in the extension of free trade and the growing interdependence of nations. And Richard Price, as optimistic as Mandeville had been cynical, equated progress with moral improvement, which he assumed to be an essential fact of history. Even Gibbon, the lord of irony, was inclined to give the idea of progress his unequivocal endorsement, for in the *Decline and Fall* (which is hardly the chronicle of progress) he reached "the pleasing conclusion that every age of the world has increased, and still increases, the real wealth, the happiness, the knowledge, and perhaps the virtue, of the human race."[14]

Gibbon's "pleasing conclusion" anticipates in tone Macaulay's "interesting and delightful" contemplation of the course of English history; and Macaulay clearly owed much to both the style and thought of the Georgians as he carried the idea of progress into Victorian culture. The mid-Victorians in turn, though influenced, as we shall see, by other progressive philosophies, share a good deal of Macaulay's frame of mind and sometimes even seem to echo his language. Buckle expected that the great history he was never to finish would demonstrate the advance of reason and the retreat of the same forces of medieval "superstition" that Macaulay had condemned. Lord Acton, though he came to repudiate Macaulay's "violent Liberalism," continued to believe progress toward greater liberty the central force in the modern world and the certain warrant of a guiding Providence throughout history.[15] Walter

Bagehot defended the notion of a "verifiable progress" to be achieved in any society once "government by discussion" had broken the bonds of outmoded custom: "Then, and then only," he wrote, "the motives which Lord Macaulay counted on to secure the progress of mankind, in fact, begin to work; *then* 'the tendency in every man to ameliorate his condition' begins to be important, because then man can alter his condition while before he is pegged down by ancient usage."[16] And Frederic Harrison, though he questioned the materialism of his time, declared in familiar accents, "The cause of progress is bound up with every principle worth having; and material progress is an indispensable step in general progress. . . . We all feel a-tiptoe with hope and confidence. . . . It is *not* the age of money-bags and cant, soot, hubbub, and ugliness. It is the age of great expectation and unwearied striving after better things."[17]

Such assertions, supported by the somewhat less emphatic avowals of Dr. Arnold, Mill, Morley, Kingsley, Huxley, and many others, reaffirmed the eighteenth-century idea of progress as a primary dogma of the Victorian period.[18] Despite their distrust of metaphysics, few of the liberal rationalists who were its most consistent and articulate proponents suspected that the notion was after all a metaphysical assumption of dubious validity, and none would have guessed the extent to which it would be repudiated by a later generation. In 1920, near the end of his scholarly career, J. B. Bury, the last of the great Victorian historians, celebrated Progress in a comprehensive survey as "the animating and controlling idea of western civilisation." Indeed, he said, "the earthly Progress of humanity is the general test to which social aims and theories are submitted as a matter of course." But in 1920 *The Decline of the West* was also appearing, and to a postwar world Spengler's gloom seemed more cogent than Bury's optimism. According to the latter only an inconceivable future would destroy the gospel of Progress: "If there were good cause," Bury speculated, "for believing that the earth would be uninhabitable in A. D. 2000 or 2100 the doctrine of Progress would lose its meaning and would automatically disappear."[19] Thirty years later, after another war, that fearsome possibility seemed less remote and incredible.

Often almost a substitute religion, or at least the sanction for a secular humanism held with great moral fervor, the idea of progress seemed to most of the late Victorian liberals—as to the eighteenth-century philosophes—quite incompatible with religious orthodoxy. And some indeed saw progress in each successive break with old dogmas. Unlike Acton, Bury thought that the idea presupposed a rejection of the concept of Providence, since, if an active Providence directed events, men by their own reason could not determine progress.[20] Dismissing the notion of original sin, W. K. Clifford identified progress with the "decline of religious belief" and the consequent "free play gained for the natural goodness of men."[21] Few of the rationalists could have been surprised when Pope Pius IX listed progress as the eightieth error in his *Syllabus Errorum* of 1864. And Huxley for one must have considered the reactionary move merely further proof that "clericalism" now and always was "the deadly enemy of science," science which was to him the sole source of light and progress. Yet Frederick Temple, who was eventually to become Archbishop of Canterbury, was not only receptive to science but also willing to argue, in the liberal *Essays and Reviews*, that we may look for a real spiritual progress "in the race taken as a whole," insofar as the cumulative power of history "transforms the human race into a colossal man, whose life reaches from the creation to the day of judgment."[22] And the earlier Victorian scientists, at any rate, gave the "progress" of research in their several areas a deeply religious significance.

At a time when "knowledge" and "natural science" were virtually synonymous terms, Tennyson asked:

> Who loves not Knowledge? Who shall rail
> Against her beauty? May she mix
> With men and prosper! Who shall fix
> Her pillars? Let her work prevail.

Yet he immediately checked his praise; Knowledge *per se*, "cut from love and faith," could be willfully unconcerned with the purposes of living:

> But on her forehead sits a fire;
> She sets her forward countenance
> And leaps into the future chance,
> Submitting all things to desire.[23]

Tennyson's question was anticipated near the beginning of the nineteenth century by Thomas Chalmers, scientist and divine, in a lecture on modern astronomy: "Who shall assign a limit to the discoveries of future ages? Who can prescribe to science her boundaries, or restrain the active and insatiable curiosity of man within the circle of his present acquirements?" But Chalmers had none of Tennyson's reservations; science could not be cut from faith; microscope and telescope alike testified to the glory of God; in the little world of the atom, no less than in the great universe in space, the Almighty found "room for the exercise of all his attributes."[24] Similar sentiments animated the Bridgewater Treatises of the eighteen thirties, scientific essays specifically "on the power, wisdom, and goodness of God, as manifested in the creation." In one of these papers Charles Bell, the anatomist, insisted that the intricate design of the human hand proved that member to be divinely predestined for its particular functions, and that countless other distinct individualities throughout the animal kingdom bore incontestable witness to the separate divine ordination of species.[25] In another, Charles Babbage, the mathematician, strove to relate miraculous breaches of continuity to the providential governance of the world and to calculate the possibilities of irregularity in natural law in order "to form a faint estimate of the magnitude of that lowest step in the chain of reasoning, which leads us up to Nature's God."[26] And in a third, William Whewell of Trinity College discussed astronomy and general physics expressly "to lead the friends of religion to look with confidence and pleasure on the progress of the physical sciences, by showing how admirably every advance in our knowledge of the universe harmonizes with the belief of a most wise and good God."[27] A few years later Robert Chambers, the first popular apologist for evolution, described "the progress of organic creation" as God's chosen method of procedure by which many forms, not separately ordained, were evolved from few: "I contemplate the whole phenomena as having been in the first place arranged in the counsels of Divine Wisdom, to take place, not only upon this sphere, but upon all the others in space, under necessary modifications, and as being carried on, from first to last, here and elsewhere, under immediate favour of the creative will or energy."[28] If Chambers often seems to be adapting his tone to an audience inclined to resist his argument, we may turn to an exact research scientist, James Prescott Joule, who, lecturing on the laws of conservation, maintained that "the sovereign will of God" guaranteed the wonderful and perfect regularity of nature. "Descending from the planetary space and firmament to the surface of our earth," said Joule, "we find a vast variety of phenomena connected with the conversion of living force and heat into one another, which speak in language which cannot be misunderstood of the wisdom and beneficence of the Great Architect of nature."[29] It would not be difficult to multiply instances of such concern among early-Victorian scientists for the religious or at least broadly philosophical bearings of their research—for the relation, that is, of scientific progress to the needs of a common spiritual and intellectual culture. It may be enough to recall that the great Michael Faraday, one of the most original thinkers in the history of British science, chose to call himself never a "physicist" (as a new jargon dictated) but, according to older and more expressive usage, a "natural philosopher."[30]

In 1841, when he opened a reading room for workers at Tamworth in Staffordshire, Sir Robert Peel, the Prime Minister, strove to forestall the possible charge that the scientific knowledge which the library was designed to propagate might be "injurious . . . to the moral or religious character of the people." On the contrary, he declared, the progress of the new sciences should actually strengthen faith by opening "new sources of conviction, . . . independent of the overwhelming force of historical testimony —independent of that assent of the heart and conscience, which instinctively discovers in the pure system of Christian Morality, the internal evidence of a divine origin."[31] Peel's remarks should have seemed quite commonplace to anyone acquainted with the Bridgewater Treatises.[32] But John Henry Newman, apparently alarmed at what seemed to him the substitution of natural for revealed religion, made the address the occasion for seven brilliant letters to *The Times* on secular knowledge as related to faith and morals. It was not, he wrote, the function of science to infer religious truths, which lay beyond the reach of mere reasoning. A teleological view demanded certain *a priori* assumptions, in themselves "unscientific." One might put the question: "Does the sun shine to warm the earth, or is the earth warmed because the sun shines?" And either hypothesis could supply the answer. To a man of religion like Sir Robert, "Science has ever suggested religious thoughts; he colours the phenomena of physics with the hues of his own mind, and mistakes an interpretation for a deduction." But to a man without an initial religious feeling, the study of nature offered only the temptation to sink into a complete atheism. "Can physics," Newman asked, "teach moral matters without ceasing to be physics?" Morality belonged to the sphere of religion, not to the world of the galvanic battery or the differential calculus. Science might indeed increase our sense of wonder, but wonder was not religion, "or we should be worshipping our railroads."[33] Newman might readily have found a good many rail-worshipers in the eighteen forties, the age of Hudson and the entrepreneurs. But he could not believe in a progress which was neither moral nor spiritual. "Progress," he once said, "is a slang term."[34] And science he left to its own devices, relieved of theological responsibility.

After 1850 Victorian scientists did in fact make less and less frequent appeals to any sort of religious sanction. Sometimes their research, like that of James Clerk Maxwell in the new physics, was too abstruse to be presented intelligibly to a general public.[35] But when they did attempt to relate their theories to a social context as the social Darwinians did, they often restated the idea of progress in secular terms. "The scientific intellect," according to Matthew

Arnold, could accept "the idea that the world is in a course
of development, of *becoming*, towards a perfection infinitely greater than we now can even conceive, the idea of a
tendance à l'ordre present in the universe 'groaning and
travailing in pain together,' " and could "willingly let the
religious instincts and the language of religion gather
around it."[36] With so bright a prospect as substitute for
the providential view of time and the future, science itself
could become virtually the object of worship. We live, said
J. R. Seeley, who had grown impatient with the old faith,
"we live under the blessed light of science, a light yet far
from its meridian and dispersing every day some noxious
superstition, some cowardice of the human spirit."[37]

But science deals quite unscientifically in value judgments, and even evolution cannot be properly equated with
progress until the attributes of advance are adequately defined. Victorian evolutionists placed a premium on the capacity to survive; but survival amidst fierce competition
was often far too immoral in its force—or at best far too
amoral—to be called progress, if the latter entailed any
moral requirement. Mill recognized the problem when he
demonstrated the fallacy of man's trying to achieve the
moral life by "following nature"; and Huxley came, at the
end of his long career as Darwin's champion, to suspect
that no biological doctrine could serve as the basis of an
ethical code. Darwin himself chose not to explore the social
implications of his theory, and he had no taste for metaphysical questions. But he did think of evolution as change
to "higher," more complex forms; he believed, according to
the conclusion of *The Origin of Species*, that "as natural
selection works solely by and for the good of each being,
all corporeal and mental endowments will tend to progress
towards perfection"; and he expected specifically, as he

wrote to Lyell, the continued improvement of the human race: "I am content that man will probably advance, and care not much whether we are looked at as mere savages in a remotely distant future."[38] Yet he failed entirely to understand Samuel Butler's insistence that real progress depended not on the blind chance of natural selection but on a *willed* evolution, a self-conscious and ultimately moral choice. He refused to consider that his own unexamined assumptions of progress, of growth "solely by and for the good," might be open to serious intellectual debate.

Huxley declared that ethics must wage a precarious warfare against darker forces in human society "as long as the world lasts." Nonetheless, he said, he could "see no limit to the extent to which intelligence and will, guided by sound principles of investigation, and organized common effort, may modify the conditions of existence, for a period longer than that now covered by history."[39] Far less cautious, Herbert Spencer looked forward to a moral as well as a material advance. Evolution, he argued, had promoted life, and life was good. Any action conducive to life-preserving was both pleasurable and moral, and man in a highly evolved society was more and more prepared to respect and further such conduct. Evolution was thus ethically good, and ethics was a moralizing process, progressive not static. "Progress, . . ." said Spencer, "is not an accident, but a necessity. . . . As surely as there is any efficacy in educational culture, or any meaning in such terms as habit, custom, practice, . . . so surely must the things we call evil and immorality disappear; so surely must man become perfect."[40] Yet the perfection would be a far-off consummation. Like Macaulay, Spencer looked not to a rapidly approaching utopia but to an indefinite continuum of progress.

In the twentieth century, when the idea of progress has declined and withered, only the scientists and the rationalists, oriented toward science, retain much of a Victorian confidence in the future. Huxley's grandson Julian, for example, continues to rejoice that Darwinism exploded the notion of "a past Golden Age" and "all static conceptions of human life," and in their stead established "inevitable change and possible progress."[41] The hope of the new biologists, insofar as they do believe in progress, turns to guided evolution, controlled reproduction, predictable progeny; but before science can even contemplate so providential a role, it must agree, as it perhaps never will, upon progressive standards, the criteria of human excellence. Bertrand Russell, pleading for the abandonment of nuclear arms, themselves the product of a highly sophisticated scientific technology, offers a glimpse of what could be a peaceful world's "reasonable expectation" of happiness: "With the progress of evolution, what is now the shining genius of an eminent few might become a common possession of the many. . . . No, let us not listen to the pessimist, for, if we do, we are traitors to Man's future. . . . Man, the latest of species, is still an infant. No limit can be set to what he may achieve in the future."[42] Yet the mood now is at best conditional, far less certain than Macaulay's or Spencer's. Julian Huxley sees progress as "possible" rather than necessary, and Lord Russell's vision of the future is but a gallant hope, made under the threat of complete disaster.

Perhaps because literature is essentially retrospective, men of letters have seldom received the idea of progress with the unqualified optimism of the rationalists and men of science. During the early nineteenth century, however, the notion seemed in general accord with the prevailing concepts of history and public time, the evidence of rapid change throughout society and the conviction that the meaning of life lay not in present achievement so much as in continued onward aspiration. And three of the major Romantic poets give the idea itself direct and memorable expression. Shelley mingles it with Godwinian perfectibility in many pieces from the callow *Queen Mab* to the great final movement of *Prometheus Unbound* or the ecstatic last chorus of *Hellas*. Keats allows Oceanus to voice the sentiment during the debate of the Titans in *Hyperion*:

> Mark well!
> As Heaven and Earth are fairer, fairer far
> Than Chaos and blank Darkness, though once chiefs;
> And as we show beyond that Heaven and Earth
> In form and shape compact and beautiful,
> In will, in action free, companionship,
> And thousand other signs of purer life;
> So on our heels a fresh perfection treads,
> A power more strong in beauty, born of us
> And fated to excel us, as we pass
> In glory that old Darkness . . .

And Wordsworth shows us how the idea, passed on to him by the French ideologists, became his own warm emotion near the beginning of the French Revolution:

> Bliss was it in that dawn to be alive,
> But to be young was very Heaven! O times,
> In which the meagre, stale, forbidding ways
> Of custom, law, and statute, took at once
> The attraction of a country in romance!
> When Reason seemed the most to assert her rights,
> When most intent on making of herself
> A prime enchantress—to assist the work,
> Which then was going forward in her name!

But Shelley's confidence alternates with a deeper despair until the time of *The Triumph of Life*, which—at least as far as it goes—seems uncompromisingly to reject the idea of progress. The argument in *Hyperion* serves a dramatic function and by no means reflects Keats's personal commitment. And Wordsworth's lines, when read in the context of *The Prelude*, attain their poignancy in large part through the past tense; they are written after the fact, and they view the lost enthusiasm from the vantage point of later disillusion. Wordsworth's mature and quite pragmatic response to progress appears in a prose letter to *The Friend*, where he rebukes the reactionaries who falsely idealize the past. "Let us allow and believe," he writes, "that there is a progress in the species towards unattainable perfection, or whether there be or not, that it is a necessity of a good and greatly-gifted nature to believe it." Even so, one need not think of the gradual progress as a steady advance on every front; the present is mixed, an alloy of much that is worthless with some "genuine merit." Yet there is, the poet concludes, "in these islands, in the departments of natural philosophy, of mechanic ingenuity, in the general activities of the country, and in the particular excellence of individual minds, in the high stations civil or military, enough to excite admiration and love in the sober-minded, and more than enough to intoxicate the youthful and inexperienced."[43] Thus the idea of progress, even if nothing more than an illusion, might act as a spur to fresh creative effort and as a wholesome admonishment that the real talents of the present should not be summarily dismissed.

Though progress became a pervasive concern in Victorian culture, none of the new poets celebrated the idea with a positive force comparable to that of the Romantics. No verses on the theme, except the rhetorical "Locksley

Hall" spoken by a dangerously excitable young man, matched the vigor of Macaulay's prose. Progress was perhaps an implicit assumption behind some of Tennyson's political pieces, where "Freedom slowly broadens down/ From precedent to precedent," or Clough's "Say Not the Struggle Nought Availeth," or Browning's "Rabbi Ben Ezra," where, in more personal terms, "The best is yet to be." But most of the poetry, including the bulk of Tennyson's, was far more likely to attack than to support the idea. Arnold as prose-writer might make occasional concessions to progressive science, but as poet he repeatedly deplored the giddy tempo and the Bacchanalian clamor of his age. Swinburne made deliberate gestures toward progress as a political ideal in *Songs before Sunrise*, but in his more spirited and spontaneous *Poems and Ballads* he exalted the "fearless old fashion" of the Ancients above all the practices of the Moderns. And James Thomson perplexed his only close friends, the ebullient secularists, by the unmitigated gloom of the unprogressive *City of Dreadful Night*. By the late-Victorian period the poets, followed by other men of letters, had made the questioning of progress so familiar a pursuit that not even the most convinced apologists for science could affirm the idea with the original naïve certainty.

❧ IV ❧

THE RECESSION OF PROGRESS

Let us hush this cry of "Forward" till ten
thousand years have gone.
                    —Tennyson

Nothing recedes like progress.
                    —E. E. Cummings

In his old age the hero of "Locksley Hall," no longer
the apologist for progress, fears that he may be accused of
"unprogressive dotage." As he speaks in the 1886 sequel,
"Locksley Hall Sixty Years After," he is scarcely more
temperate than the young man of the monologue published
forty-four years before. Yet there is still method in his
heated rhetoric; and the aged Tennyson, who is not wholly
concealed by the dramatic mask, rightly considered that
the companion pieces would one day be thought "two of
the most historically interesting of his poems"[1] as com-
mentaries on the changing temper of his times. Whereas
the first casts the optimism of Macaulay's generation in
memorable rhyme, the second reflects a common late-Victorian disillusion. The cry of "Forward" has been "lost
within a growing gloom" until it seems delusive and irrelevant: "Let us hush this cry of 'Forward' till ten thousand
years have gone." Mechanical advances, including the rail-

way and the steamship, have become familiar and void of
wonder and yet have not changed the quality of human
life:

> Half the marvels of my morning, triumphs over
>   time and space,
> Staled by frequence, shrunk by usage into a
>   commonest commonplace!

The old dreams of a perfected world, without war or disease, a world cultivated like a paradisal garden, are mocked
by the nightmare vision of vastly multiplied populations
struggling hungrily for survival. Evolution as improvement
appears to be constantly contending with retrogression—

> Evolution ever climbing after some ideal good,
> And Reversion ever dragging Evolution in the mud.

And the course of Time is seen to swerve unsteadily and
"turn upon itself in many a backward streaming curve."
Progress has been freely identified with the way of Science,
and Science continues its confident exploration, but, the
old man asks, has there been a truly comparable social development?

> Is it well that while we range with Science,
>   glorying in the Time,
> City children soak and blacken soul and sense
>   in city slime?

And the city itself with its mean streets and sordid "war-
rens of the poor" is all the answer the question requires:
"There among the glooming alleys Progress halts on palsied
feet."

   Earlier in the eighties Henry George was lecturing to
the Victorians in very similar terms, though in the drier

measured tones of the economist, and his great work, *Progress and Poverty*, at first ignored in America, was rapidly finding a large responsive English audience. "Where the conditions," George wrote, "to which material progress everywhere tends are most fully realized—that is to say, where population is densest, wealth greatest, and the machinery of production and exchange most highly developed —we find the deepest poverty, the sharpest struggle for existence, and the most of enforced idleness. . . . The 'tramp' comes with the locomotive, and almshouses and prisons are as surely the marks of 'material progress' as are costly dwellings, rich warehouses, and magnificent churches. . . . The enormous increase in productive power which has marked the present century and is still going on with accelerating ratio . . . simply widens the gulf between Dives and Lazarus. . . . This association of poverty with progress is the great enigma of our times." The hero of the first "Locksley Hall" had chosen to remain an Englishman "in the foremost files of time," rather than take unto himself, as he had madly dreamed of doing, a "squalid savage" mate on some lonely South Sea isle. But George could now declare his firm belief that any man, if he had his choice at birth, would be infinitely wiser to choose the lot of a savage than life "among the lowest classes in such a highly civilized country as Great Britain."[2] (Tennyson's hero, of course, was in no danger of sinking so low in the scale.) Poverty was nothing new to England, but to present it as a necessary concomitant of modern progress was to make a fresh assault on the complacency of those comfortably "glorying in the Time." Though George's remedy, the single tax, might be hotly disputed, few could deny the skill of his diagnosis.

There were, however, other grounds for questioning progress, reasons quite unrelated to the tangible evidence of social unrest and injustice in the late-Victorian period. Years before *Progress and Poverty* Mill had shocked his liberal disciples by "an audacious doubt" that all the mechanical inventions of the century had substantially enriched the life of any man.[3] But eventually most of the rationalists shared some of his misgivings. Morley came to feel that material prosperity could impair "the moral and intellectual nerve" and later to wonder whether it were more than an "optimist superstition" to believe "that civilised communities are universally bound somehow or another to be progressive."[4] Huxley in one of his last essays commented on the decline of "modern speculative optimism" with its notions of perfectibility and progress: "One does not," he wrote, "hear so much of it as one did forty years ago; indeed, I imagine it is to be met with more commonly at the tables of the healthy and wealthy, than in the congregations of the wise."[5] And Harrison—though like George he saw the horrors of the modern industrial metropolis and the continuing degradation of the poor—was alarmed that the cult of progress was destroying the peace and sanity of even the relatively comfortable. Suppose, he speculated, that after a few more technological advances we were able, like Jules Verne's heroes, to explore outer space, holiday on the moon, "hold scientific meetings in the nebulae of Orion": we should then "seem to one another madmen," for we should have sacrificed all point of rest, affection, and fellowship to mere mobility. "Rest and fixity," he concluded, "are essential to thought, to social life, to beauty; and a growing series of mechanical inventions making life a string of dissolving views is a bar to rest and to fixity of any sort."[6] Material progress might thus menace the true objects of humanity.

Besides, as Tennyson suggested, reversion no less than advance might be a fact of history; or—as Huxley put it, in terms of biological evolution—"Retrogressive is as practicable as progressive metamorphosis."[7] The new archaeology, which seemed at one moment to be offering a testimony of steady progress, at the next was furnishing incontestable proof of social retrogression.[8] Prehistoric cave-painting, charged with a rich creative energy, had flourished widely, then disappeared altogether, and its power had not been matched in art for millennia. "Thronèd races" (to use the language of *In Memoriam*) had clearly degraded; and whole civilizations had vanished —not necessarily to make way for higher cultures. Perhaps the metaphor of ebb-and-flow, most memorably developed in Arnold's "Dover Beach," was more adequate a description of the movement of public time than the image of a resolute forward march. Even those who normally assumed the reality of progress could picture to themselves recessive and resurgent social tides. George Eliot, for example, though intellectually aligned with the progressive radicals, wrote to her friend Mme. Bodichon in December 1859, when the latter had remarked that France in a martial mood might attack England: "It is depressing to witness this reaction towards barbarism. One would like one's life to be borne on the onward wave and not the receding one —the flow and not the ebb: yet somebody must live in the bad times, and there is no reason, I suppose, out of our own esteem for ourselves, why the best things in the lot of mankind should fall to us in particular."[9] Others, like Arnold, heard in the long withdrawing roar of the tide only a

denial that the assumption of real progress had either validity or meaning.

By the eighties continued advance in knowledge, especially in the natural sciences, demanded increasingly spe-
cialized research, concentration upon smaller and smaller
units to the necessary exclusion of more general concerns.
Though such progress opened many new areas of fact and
theory, it taxed both the specialist and the society he lived
in; it tended, as Harrison claimed, to sap "all grip and
elasticity of mind"[10] and so to militate against broadly
humanistic discourse among educated men. It marked the
advent of professionalism, which in the last two decades of
the century, according to Whitehead, brought "one of the
dullest phases of thought since the time of the First Cru-
sade."[11] If the specialist lacked ability to relate or apply his
limited work to the community as a whole, the specific
little progress he had achieved might diminish rather than
increase a larger progress; by isolating each expert from his
fellows, the new professionalism meant a fragmentation of
general culture.

Still the progress in science, even if atomistic in effect,
was at least demonstrable; the new discovery, however
small, stood as a distinct contribution to the field. In social
matters, on the other hand, new developments might be
seen from one point of view as progressive, from another
as disruptive. The spread of free public instruction, for
instance, could dilute the quality of education; the increase
in the rate of literacy could bring a decrease in the substance of literature. Whereas some, like Huxley, thought
every rebuke to "clericalism" a victory for the human
spirit, others, both within and without the church, saw
symptoms of cultural decadence in the widespread challenge to religious orthodoxy. Each successive extension of

the franchise was held to be both salutary and disastrous. In the eighties and nineties the liberals hailed the new feminism, and the conservatives, many of them women, deplored the disappearance of the womanly virtues and the woeful unsexing of society. Meanwhile, the new imperialism was promising to extend British progress to the ends of the earth or, alternately, foretelling the disintegration of the Victorian hegemony. "The elements of progress and decline," said Ruskin, were "strangely mingled in the modern mind."[12]

In much of his early work, especially in *Heart of Darkness* and *Nostromo*, Joseph Conrad was concerned with the moral ambiguities of a progress linked to self-interest and the imperialistic exploitation of uncivilized peoples. "Progress," he said, "leaves its dead by the way, for progress is only a great adventure as its leaders and chiefs know very well in their hearts. It is a march into an undiscovered country, and in such an enterprise the victims do not count."[13] This precisely is the attitude of Travers, the ruthless jingo of *The Rescue*, who deludes himself into defending the logic of genocide: "And if the inferior race must perish, it is a gain, a step towards the perfecting of humanity which is the aim of progress."[14] When such crimes could be committed, or at least rationalized, in the name of progress, we should not wonder that Conrad and other men of moral imagination came to look upon the idea itself with profound distrust.

It was perhaps inevitable in any case that the most convinced progressive philosophers should alienate any artist. The Comtean Positivists—and many others who accepted Comte's general assumptions, though not necessarily his rigid dogmas—believed that society, having outgrown the theological and metaphysical stages, had already progressed to its third phase, the positive or scientific—"In the first, the mind invents; in the second, it abstracts; in the third, it submits itself to positive facts."[15] In other words, poetry, all creative art, belonged to the lost childhood of the race. If progress was to be equated with the accumulation of the positive facts of science, the artist by the late nineteenth century might very well prefer to look back to a more manageable past, for the new sciences were presenting a world of inhuman vastness and of little apparent harmony or purpose.

On a more immediate level, applied or practical science was expressing itself in terms of an unprecedented industrial progress which seemed wholly at odds with all aesthetic impulse. "Science grows and Beauty dwindles," complained the old man of the second "Locksley Hall," "—roofs of slated hideousness." The architectural reference suggests Morris' long campaign against ugly building and reconstruction and, perhaps, more specifically, anticipates a letter, written a year before his death, in which Morris professed to be "quite sickened" by the sight of a new roof on a picturesque old barn.[16] And the epithet recalls Arnold's indictment of London—"London, with its unutterable external hideousness, and with its internal canker of *publicē egestas, privatim opulentia*—to use the words which Sallust puts into Cato's mouth about Rome—unequalled in all the world!"[17] Hopkins saw much of the landscape befouled by industry, "seared with trade, bleared, smeared with toil," wearing "man's smudge." And Ruskin, convinced that "the peculiar forces of devastation induced by modern city life" had only lately entered the world, said that he could find no language strong enough "to describe the forms of filth, and modes of ruin" that had sullied what had once been a

green and pleasant country lane.[18] To Ruskin, and indeed
to all these others, urban squalor, suburban drabness, the
unloveliness of smoke-filled valleys and polluted streams
were outward marks of an inner malady; the aesthetic
estimate was prelude to a moral judgment. It seemed difficult to dissociate industrial progress from social decadence.
Possibly, thought Arnold, the future would achieve some
"solemn peace of its own," but the present prospect was
bleak and forbidding to the poet:

> And we say that repose has fled
> Forever the course of the River of Time.
> That cities will crowd to its edge
> In a blacker incessanter line;
> That the din will be more on its banks,
> Denser the trade on its stream,
> Flatter the plain where it flows,
>   Fiercer the sun overhead.
> That never will those on its breast
> See an ennobling sight,
> Drink of the feeling of quiet again.[19]

Nonetheless, despite all misgivings, Arnold continued
throughout his life to value the pursuit of perfection and
even to believe in some sort of spiritual advance. He carefully distinguished between a man's true "progress in sweetness and light" and "the number of the railroads he has
constructed, or the bigness of the tabernacle he has built."[20]
And he conceded that even the lesser progress might at last
reach some happier issue: "Then, too, in spite of all that
is said about the absorbing and brutalising influence of our
passionate material progress, it seems to me indisputable
that this progress is likely, though not certain, to lead in the
end to an apparition of intellectual life; and that man, after
he has made himself perfectly comfortable and has now to

determine what to do with himself next, may begin to remember that he has a mind, and that the mind may be made the source of great pleasure."[21] His early poem "Progress" admits the possibility of fruitful change in religion, yet cautions against the hasty repudiation of long-established creeds and attitudes. For this was the source of Arnold's dissatisfaction with the doctrinaire apostles of intellectual progress: his own need of the past, his respect as artist for conventions and traditions that a self-righteous progressive age felt free to ignore.

At the beginning of the Victorian period, Carlyle had expressed a similar ambivalence in his challenging of nineteenth-century assumptions. He had admired the initiative of the Captains of Industry but deplored the progressive course of unbridled industrialism. He had denied that history could or should repeat itself, yet had demanded that the best of the past be cherished and preserved by constant metamorphosis. "I do not make much of 'Progress of the Species,' as handled in these times of ours," he told the audience at his lectures on heroes, "nor do I think you would care to hear much about it. The talk on that subject is too often of the most extravagant, confused sort." Still it was obvious, he went on, that there must be some sort of forward movement in society; for "absolutely without originality there is no man. No man whatever believes, or can believe, exactly what his grandfather believed; he enlarges somewhat, by fresh discovery, his view of the Universe, and consequently his Theorem of the Universe. . . . It is the history of every man; and in the history of Mankind we see it summed-up into great historical amounts,—revolutions, new epochs."[22] Sentiments so qualified, though more positive than Carlyle's later views, were already far removed from Macaulay's naïve faith and "most extravagant" talk.

By the end of the period the idea of progress had altogether lost its authority among the poets and writers of imaginative prose. But enough of the concept still remained to provide occasional irony, point of contrast, or even theme. Hardy, for example, could not forgive the progress that was destroying old legend, folklore, and rustic individuality, and his depiction of the lives of rural workers grew increasingly pessimistic as he brought their story down to nearly contemporary times, when their lot actually had much improved.[23] Yet he was almost ready to believe that his darkling thrush was greeting the new century with some blessed Hope, whereof he himself was unaware. In *Jude the Obscure* his protagonist assumes both the idea of progress and its reverse; Jude tells Sue that their advanced ideas are "fifty years too soon"; yet he agrees with the doctor that little Father Time's murderous conduct represents "the beginning of the coming universal wish not to live."[24] Though Hardy liked to call himself a meliorist, his own attitude, even at its least negative, was shadowed and ambiguous.

But it is to Kipling that we should turn for a last ironic comment. Fascinated by machines and uniquely able to describe their rhythms, Kipling understood to the full the power of the new technology that was the mainspring of material progress. But in "The Bridge-Builders," a long short story published in 1898, he pitted that power against a stronger and more enduring force. His hero Findlayson, an English engineer, has almost completed what he hopes will be the great and lasting work of his lifetime, a bridge over the Ganges, when raging floods threaten to loosen the piers and sweep away the whole superstructure. Adrift in a small boat and feverish, he accepts an opium dose from an Indian co-worker and, heavily drugged, lapses into a nightmare which admits him to the council of the ancient river-gods who are affronted by his ugly insolent contrivance. At length, dazed yet preternaturally receptive, he learns the gods' decision: the bridge may stand as an object temporary and inconsequential, since the duration of human things, after all, by the gods' reckoning, is ludicrously brief. The delusions of strength and progress are scarcely worth serious consideration. But Findlayson, when he recovers daylight and reason, cannot afford to remember such truths; his first concern in the morning is that his bridge has survived; and the ageless ominous voices from the past may be conveniently forgotten.

In questioning progress the poets and novelists were not necessarily eager to repudiate the idea altogether; few would have wished, like Tennyson's elderly spokesman, to hush the cry of forward for the next ten thousand years. They sought rather to explore the content and implications of the assumption and, in specific instances, to define the quality of alleged improvements, to ask whether the particular innovation was worth the price it had cost society as a whole in terms of real culture. They deplored the indifference of the progressive scientific mind to the values of a past often rich beyond the present in art and ideas. And, above all, they denied that headlong movement for its own sake, the mere acceleration of tempo which some of their contemporaries considered the very essence of progress, could be of real human or humanistic worth; for men, if they were actually to advance, must always, they felt, have the capacity to withdraw, to reflect, to view all movement in due perspective. Ruskin early in his long career was speaking for the best in the Victorian imagination when he attacked the fallacy of speed. "We shall be obliged at last," he said, "to confess, what we should long ago have known, that the really precious things are thought and sight, not pace. . . . It does . . . a man, if he be truly a man, no harm to go slow; for his glory is not at all in going, but in being."[25]

✒ V ✑

THE IDEA OF DECADENCE

> Evening strains to be tíme's vást, / womb-of-
> all, home-of-all, hearse-of-all night. . . .
> Heart, you round me right
> With: Óur évening is over us; óur night /
> whélms, whélms, ánd will end us.
> –Hopkins

In the winter of 1898 Joseph Conrad complained of the dying sun. But his concern was more cosmic than seasonal. "The fate of a humanity condemned ultimately to perish from cold," he wrote to his friend Cunninghame Graham, "is not worth troubling about. If you take it to heart it becomes an unendurable tragedy. If you believe in improvement you must weep, for the attained perfection must end in cold, darkness and silence."[1] Twelve years earlier Tennyson had allowed the speaker of the second "Locksley Hall" to contemplate the dead moon with similar bitterness:

> Dead the new astronomy calls her, . . .
>
> Dead, but how her living glory lights the hall, the
> dune, the grass!
> Yet the moonlight is the sunlight, and the sun
> himself will pass.

In more precise terms, the science that prompted both comments arose largely from the researches of William Thomson, Lord Kelvin. Despite technicalities beyond the grasp of most men of letters, the new astrophysics deeply stirred the literary imagination of the late nineteenth century.

As early as 1852 Thomson had helped formulate the second law of thermodynamics, according to which the sum of useful energy throughout the universe would be constantly reduced by the diffusion of heat until all had reached a state of entropy. "Within a finite period of time past," he had concluded, "the earth must have been, and within a finite period to come, the earth must again be, unfit for the habitation of man as at present constituted."[2] The general implications of the law, however, were not spelled out in popular terms till twenty years later when Balfour Stewart, professor of physics at Owens College, Manchester, issued his "elementary treatise" on the conservation of energy. "Universally diffused heat," said Stewart, "forms what we may call the great waste-heap of the universe, and this is growing larger year by year. . . . We are led to look to an end in which the whole universe will be one equally heated inert mass, and from which everything like life or motion or beauty will have utterly gone away."[3] In other words, according to assured scientific theory, human time eventually must have a stop. H. G. Wells's time-traveler, returning from the remote future, could therefore report on the earth's bleak last days. And Hardy's Tess could tell her little brother, gazing at the starry sky, that we lived on a "blighted" world. Whereas the new biology had seemed, at least for a while, to fortify a belief in progress, the new physics apparently denied the possibility of any such faith. Many a knowing late Victorian could have understood Conrad's lament: "If you believe in improvement you must weep."

In America Henry Adams specifically cited the second

law of thermodynamics as the point of departure for his own "physical theory of history," and he saw in it a sanction for his brother Brooks's *Law of Civilization and Decay*, which appeared in London in 1895. Brooks was convinced that crude money-interests had squandered the vital energies of society and made certain its disintegration. "The elasticity of the age of expansion," he insisted, had already gone, and the general contraction of real culture had begun.[4] Yet if such an argument assumed a scientific parallel, time was running to its end much more rapidly for the Adamses than for the physicists. Henry, drawing a dubious analogy to ancient Rome (he found "an astonishing parity" between Brooks and the elder Pliny), and making due allowance for his own notion of acceleration, calculated that "we ought still to have more than two hundred years of futile and stupid stagnation," and added wearily, "I find twenty too much for me."[5] The decline of the West at the close of the nineteenth century might thus be set, with all solemnity, against the death of the universe in aeons yet to come.

On the other hand, the idea of decadence could also seek immediate scientific support. Ruskin late in his career was more troubled by Victorian geology than by the new physics. His reading of Lyell, he said, convinced him that there were three great periods in geological history: that in which the earth was crystallized, that in which it was "sculptured," and "that in which it is now being unsculptured, or deformed." Earth accordingly was now in its "decrepitude"; glaciers were no longer cutting deeply but merely piling up debris, and "all mountain forms [were] suffering a deliquescent and corroding change."[6] Though Ruskin's knowledge of science was rather more precise than Adams's, his use of data was no less subjective;[7] the evidence he presented was clearly intended to harmonize with his notion of a social and moral disintegration. If science, as in the Bridgewater Treatises, was expected in the eighteen thirties to justify the ways of God to men, toward the end of the century it seemed to be merely another source of a deepening pessimism, or at least no cause for renewed confidence. For the scientist, even if not prepared to think of the world as already in its decrepitude, could no longer consider the universe forever young and inexhaustible. Huxley, who summed up much of the best in scientific thought, was thus forced to qualify his most sanguine prediction; the possibilities of advance and discovery would be great for many years, but not indefinitely, only indeed "until the evolution of our globe shall have entered so far upon its downward course that the cosmic process resumes its sway, and, once more, the State of Nature prevails over the surface of our planet."[8]

The idea of decadence, however, was far older than any of the new scientific sanctions it could find in the late Victorian period. Indeed it antedated by centuries the idea of progress, which gave the first real stimulus to all modern science. Nostalgia for a lost and better past bulks large in classical literature. The Greeks postulated a bygone golden age, the idealities of which furnished standards for measuring the shortcomings of the present. The Romans, especially Horace and Cicero, lamented the moral and political degeneration of their own times. The Hebrew and Christian traditions accounted for human depravity by the story of the fall and the doctrine of original sin; and the decay of the world as a consequence of man's first defection persisted as a literary theme through the Renaissance. In eighteenth-century France and England, where the idea of progress was gaining wide currency, the idea of decadence also aroused considerable speculation. Montesquieu and Gibbon were alike concerned to determine the causes of the decline and fall of Rome. Volney in *Les Ruines* warned that ignorance, superstition, and the love of wealth could destroy empires; and Rousseau argued that progress, insofar as it involved luxury, necessarily brought decadence in its train. By the seventeen eighties a number of social critics, both English and French, were finding European society sadly decadent by comparison with the new nation born of the American Revolution. Meanwhile, for many years architects had been preserving or creating actual ruins as sentimental adjuncts of an ordered landscape, reminders of life's brevity and time's cruel ravages, a means of titillating the poetic sensibilities of men otherwise devoted to practical prose and reason.

Nonetheless, familiar though it may have been to earlier eras, the idea of decadence grew steadily more urgent and immediate throughout the Victorian age (and simultaneously, for somewhat different reasons, during the Second Empire in France). Decadence was no longer simply an aspect of the common death that fallen man was heir to; it was a morbid condition of the social psyche, a disease sapping the vitality of civilization. In retrospect, the Victorians, for all their misgivings and uncertainties, their mixed response to science and their religious doubts, may seem to us relatively sheltered, free from the threat of catastrophic global conflict, free to realize their individualities in a secure and prosperous society. Yet they felt the menace of time almost as much as its promise; and the comfortable notion of progress was often forced to do battle with the darker concept of decadence. At the end of the age, A. J. Balfour, one of the most philosophic of its statesmen, strove to define the idea. "When through an ancient and still powerful state," he wrote, "there spreads a mood of deep discouragement, when the reaction against recurring ills grows feebler, and the ship rises less buoyantly to each succeeding wave, when learning languishes, enterprise slackens and vigour ebbs away, then, as I think, there is present some process of social degeneration, which we must perforce recognise, and which, pending a satisfactory analysis, may conveniently be distinguished by the name of 'decadence.' "[9] Though his terms are general, Balfour seems clearly to have based his deduction on a specific regard for his own time and country. If the ship of state was scarcely foundering, many an observer at the close of the century yet felt that it was weathering the storm with decreased buoyancy. But long before the vigor of the economy could be questioned, a mood of discouragement, from many sources, had begun to pervade Victorian thought and letters; a deep malaise recurred throughout the whole period till at last among intellectuals it became a principal element in the modern temper.

In 1834, setting out for the Middle East, which he was to describe in his genial *Eothen*, the young Alexander Kinglake denounced the "stale civilisation" of the West.[10] Many of the later Victorian travelers—notably David Livingstone, Laurence Oliphant, Richard Burton, Wilfrid Blunt, and C. M. Doughty—must have felt a similar impatience with the middle-class respectabilities. But neither Kinglake nor these others (except perhaps Oliphant, who eventually founded his own eccentric new order) considered the "stale" society of England really degenerate or decadent. And assuredly Macaulay, the apostle of progress, did not. Yet even he could imagine a condition worse than staleness, a remote time of complete collapse when a visitor from

New Zealand might, "in the midst of a vast solitude, take his stand on a broken arch of London Bridge to sketch the ruins of St. Paul's."[11]

Less sanguine souls could see the evil days nearer at hand. Froude declared in the eighteen sixties: "We live in times of disintegration, and none can tell what will be after us."[12] Ruskin in the next decade announced with assurance: "The British nation is at present unhealthy, poor, and likely to perish, as a power, from the face of the earth."[13] Hopkins near the end of the eighties, in one of his last and grimmest sonnets, complained that economic injustice was already the blighting "curse of our times":

> This, by Despair, bred Hangdog dull; by Rage,
> Manwolf, worse; and their packs infest the age.[14]

And Morris soon afterwards, or at least the "I" of Nowhere, remarked that only in the utopia could he enjoy art with an easy conscience: "For the first time in my life, I was having my fill of the pleasure of the eyes without any of that sense of incongruity, that dread of approaching ruin, which had always beset me hitherto when I had been amongst the beautiful works of art of the past."[15] In his own age Morris considered all art "doomed" since it was the expression of an unjust and moribund social system. And he was quite prepared to see the old society perish altogether, if its death brought a release of vital energies. "I have no more faith," he said, "than a grain of mustard seed in the future of 'civilization,' which I *know* now is doomed to destruction, and probably before very long: what a joy it is to think of! and how often it consoles me to think of barbarism once more flooding the world, and real feelings and passions, however rudimentary, taking the place of our wretched hypocrisies. . . . I used really to despair once because I thought what the idiots of our day call progress would go on perfecting itself: happily I know now that all that will have a sudden check. . . ."[16]

Few could have joined Morris in welcoming the prospect of a new barbarism to supersede Victorian Britain; for to most the possibility of decadence was a source of deep anxiety. Richard Jefferies, for example, though he also sought to free the life of the heart from wretched hypocrisies, drew a forbidding sketch of a barbaric future. His *After London; or Wild England*, which Morris read with some satisfaction[17] on its appearance in 1885, has long since been a deservedly forgotten novel; yet it may still serve as a reminder of late-Victorian fears. The England it pictures has been completely decentralized and largely depopulated; mysterious tidal waves have laid waste much of the terrain, and the cities have all burned and fallen into ruins. Most of the men and women who survive have been reduced to the state of serfs terrorized by brutish masters and predatory wild animals; nearly all are illiterate and distrustful of the very few books that remain. London has become "a vast stagnant swamp," any attempt to explore which is thwarted by foul and fatal vapors. "For," we are told, "all the rottenness of a thousand years and of many hundred millions of human beings is there festering under the stagnant water, which has sunk down into and penetrated the earth, and floated up to the surface the contents of the buried cloacae."[18] The landscape, in short, is permanently polluted, and the whole realm, as at the end of Tennyson's *Idylls*, "reels back into the beast."

Tennyson indeed, more seriously than Jefferies, dreaded the encroachment of the wasteland which was both the state of a nature red in tooth and claw, and also the inner condition of brutish passion and lawless desire. From the

beginning, when he wrote lugubrious boyish pieces on the
fall of Jerusalem and the destruction of Babylon, he was
concerned with social and moral decadence. In "Oenone"
he made the defeat of reason an augury of the collapse of
Troy. In *In Memoriam* he imagined a violence which
spelled disaster,

> The fortress crashes from on high,
> The brute earth lightens to the sky,
> And the great Aeon sinks in blood.

His "Lucretius" placed the suicide of the philosopher
against the dissolution of the Republic, "the lust of blood /
That makes a steaming slaughter-house of Rome," the
Commonwealth, "which breaks / As I am breaking now!"
And the late "Tiresias," designed to have relevance to contemporary England, warned of the imminent doom of
Thebes. But the *Idylls of the King*, above all, proved as a
completed sequence the most trenchant and best sustained
treatment of social decline in Victorian poetry. Having
rapidly described the triumph of Camelot over the barbaric
wilderness, the *Idylls* analyzes at length the forces of decadence that undermine the city-state: the failure of ideal-
ism, the substitution of self-interest for civic virtue, the
decay of manners, the surrender of reason to sensuality
(suggested by the omnipresent beast imagery). When a
first generation has assured the basic security of the kingdom, a second begins to question the authority of the King,
whose ideal standard must be taken on trust, and to follow
the bad example of the Queen, whose adultery commits her
to a life of miserable deception. For most of the knights
the Grail quest is but an escape from immediate social responsibilities in an effort to achieve an unearned spiritual
satisfaction, and the few who return to Camelot come back

dejectedly to a crumbling city, "heaps of ruin, hornless unicorns, / Crack'd basilisks, and splinter'd cockatrices"; the culture that is not daily reaffirmed cannot long survive. Tristram, unabashed opportunist that he is, explains the logic of the late-comer who finds he has no need to pay more than lip-reverence to the faith upon which the civilization was originally built:

"Fool, I came late, the heathen wars were o'er,
The life had flown, we sware but by the shell . . . ."

The fair appearance for a while belies the essential emptiness; Camelot eventually falls, destroyed by what is false within. Though the settings of the separate Idylls reflect the cycle of the seasons, the implication of the poem as a whole is not that decadence must supplant cultural vigor as inevitably as autumn and winter follow summer. The fate of Camelot is not predestined; it depends on the will of the citizenry, the free decision to respond or not to the changing challenge of the time. The epilogue to the sequence makes this moral, as well as its application to Victorian Britain, only too explicit; the poet hopes that "Heaven / Will blow the tempest in the distance back" and that those alarmed by "signs of storm" may be mistaken (though he himself is not at all sure), for

—if our slowly-grown
And crown'd Republic's crowning common-sense,
That sav'd her many times, not fail—their fears
Are morning shadows huger than the shapes
That cast them, not those gloomier which forego
The darkness of that battle in the west
Where all of high and holy dies away.[19]

Matthew Arnold as a young man apparently believed that the decline of the West had already begun. His "Memorial

Verses" of 1850 to Wordsworth described Goethe, who had died eighteen years before, as "Physician of the iron age," one who

> look'd on Europe's dying hour
> Of fitful dream and feverish power;
> His eye plunged down the weltering strife,
> The turmoil of expiring life—
> He said: *The end is everywhere,*
> *Art still has truth, take refuge there!*

And Wordsworth, the elegy continued, also sensed the decadence, for

> He too upon a wintry clime
> Had fallen—on this iron time
> Of doubts, disputes, distractions, fears.

His "Youth of Nature," still on Wordsworth, repeated the theme two years later:

> He grew old in an age he condemn'd.
> He look'd on the rushing decay
> Of the times which had shelter'd his youth;
> Felt the dissolving throes
> Of a social order he loved. . . .
>
> He is dead, and the fruit-bearing day
> Of his race is past on the earth;
> And darkness returns to our eyes.

And his lyric "Revolutions" of about the same date widened the discussion to suggest that intimations of inadequacy had reached many cultures on the eve of their decline:

> And Empire after Empire, at their height
> Of sway, have felt this boding sense come on.
> Have felt their huge frames not constructed right,
> And droop'd, and slowly died upon their throne.

Empedocles on Etna sought to gain perspective by setting a quite modern decadence in ancient Sicily, where "all / Clouds and grows daily worse" and the philosopher can complain that

> The brave, impetuous heart yields everywhere
> To the subtle, contriving head;
> Great qualities are trodden down,
> And littleness united
> Is become invincible.

But the fault in *Empedocles*, as the young Callicles insists, may lie in the man as much as the age:

> 'Tis not the times, 'tis not the sophists vex him;
> There is some root of suffering in himself,
> Some secret and unfollow'd vein of woe,
> Which makes the time look black and sad to him.

Arnold himself recognized the confusion and for fifteen years suppressed the poem; his hero, denouncing the sickly thought of his world yet sinking into his own no more productive introspections, was scarcely heroic, and the action, or rather inaction, of the drama could inspirit no one; the modern "dialogue of the mind with itself," discouraged, self-pitying, antisocial, seemed as decadent as the society from which Empedocles was alienated. In his work after 1860, mostly in prose, Arnold was more constructive and even on occasion optimistic; though he still assailed the evils of society, he suggested practical remedies, or at least attitudes of mind that might devise reasonable reforms. And when forced, as in "The Function of Criticism at the Present Time," to deny the possibility of a true culture in his own iron age, he could beg his fellow-Victorians to keep alive the vision of a brighter future.

In New York Arnold told the saving remnant that, by clinging resolutely to its sober Anglo-Saxon, Puritan heritage, the United States might escape the decadence of France, which had sold itself, body and soul, to the goddess of lubricity. Yet, we may object, if lasciviousness were the chief cause of decline, Rome would have perished centuries before the barbarians swooped down upon the Christian and relatively moral community.[20] Whatever the status of sensuality in nineteenth-century France, Paris was in fact, through all political vicissitudes, the art capital of Europe, as rich in creative energy as it had ever been in its long history. Nonetheless, many of the artists themselves subscribed to the idea of decadence, though hardly with Arnold's sanctions. The sense of social dissolution was associated in their minds with nearly a century of public shocks, defeats, and disappointments: the violence of 1789, the debacle at Waterloo, the coming of the lesser Napoleon and his reactionary Second Empire, the disaster of 1871. These were actual events of magnitude, certain to leave their mark on the sensibility of the nation. And they had obviously no parallel in England, the England victorious in 1815 and free from large-scale military engagement till the late nineties, dedicated to the principles of liberty and liberalism, the voice of progress and at least until 1870 the unquestioned leader in commerce and industry. Yet the notion of decadence, as we have seen, was no more a stranger to Victorian England than to France.

At first the assumption, as in the young Arnold and the Tennyson of *In Memoriam*, was related in part to an anxious regard for revolutionary developments in politics and religion on the Continent. But by the later Victorian period there were solid reasons for uneasiness in Britain itself. After the defeat of France, Germany rapidly superseded

Britain as the dominant industrial power in Europe, and by 1914 Germany's industrial potential was equal to that of Britain and France combined. Though industry was still strong, the rate of expansion steadily declined. Bad harvests in the late seventies virtually wrecked British agriculture. Rising imports and falling exports produced an unfavorable balance of trade. Unexpectedly severe economic depressions in each of the last three decades of the century brought financial crises that sorely tried Victorian self-confidence. Prosperity at home, less assured now even in good times, depended largely on the enormous investments of British capital abroad, but "in export of capital, too, the main tide of expansionism was ebbing by the late 'seventies."[21] All of these general conditions and their immediate consequences—widespread unemployment, demonstrations, and strikes—inevitably engendered or increased a suspicion that the great day of Britain's supremacy was passing.

Writing in 1890, Havelock Ellis was convinced that the material decline might have its benefits. When no longer the center of industry, England would become "a museum of antiquities" and a sort of shrine, "a Holy Land for the whole English-speaking race." The reverence, he thought, would steadily grow: "This emotional attitude will develop mightily with the development of English-speaking nations, and will but be strengthened by the dying down of England's political and commercial activity."[22] Seventy-five years later, after ordeals and reverses more considerable than Ellis ever could have imagined, England, though reduced in wealth and influence, remains a home of art and original research, a magnificent museum indeed, but also a place of life and new ideas. Recently, however, Arnold Toynbee has suggested that, despite the obvious decline of the state, most Englishmen are now better off materially than in the age of power and imperial glory. To this his son, feeling less detached, has replied pertinently: "Strangely enough, I think many working-class people would rather be poor so long as they knew they were still on top of the world as a nation."[23] The sense of decadence, in short, is not to be equated simply with a decrease in material assets.

Many of the Victorians believed on the contrary that material success was fraught with danger. At the end of the period Henley, in a specious attempt to justify the South African war, complained that, until conflict comes,

> the nation, in a dream
> Of money and love and sport, hangs at the paps
> Of well-being, and so
> Goes fattening, mellowing, dozing, rotting down
> Into a rich deliquium of decay.[24]

Fifty years earlier the young Rossetti was able to suggest, with considerably greater subtlety, that a complacent faith in materialism invited an ultimately ruinous reckoning. In "The Burden of Nineveh" he recorded his impressions of a winged god brought from newly excavated Nineveh to the British Museum: the ominous creature, part-human, part-beast, earthbound, proud, sensual, seemed an appropriate idol not only for the ancient city that perished in its pomp and circumstance, but also—and more certainly—for nineteenth-century London, or so it might appear to archaeologists of some distant future coming upon it among the English ruins; and even now the poet, as if from beyond time, could ask incredulously,

> O Nineveh, was this thy God—
> Thine also, mighty Nineveh?

Ruskin, when invited to help design a stock exchange at Bradford, named the presiding deity of the enterprise the "Goddess of Getting-on" and warned the merchants that their religion was doomed, since the days of the goddess were numbered. And Pater, in *Marius*, with his own age clearly in mind, depicted the material opulence of the Rome of Marcus Aurelius as a prelude to a general social decline, insofar as it offered but a showy substitute for the values which must sustain a reasonable and humane culture. Indeed, much of the wealth of late Victorian England, like that of imperial Rome, was drawn from the far reaches of the empire; and the cult of imperialism served frequently to divert attention from troublesome political and moral issues in the domestic economy. As early as 1878 Gladstone insisted that his countrymen had overextended themselves, for "the cares and calls of the British Empire are already beyond the strength of those who govern and have governed it."[25] The tide of jingoism, however, mounted steadily throughout the eighties and nineties till it reached a peak in the "foolish pride and frantic boast" of the Diamond Jubilee celebrations. There the lavish and desperate display so reminded Kipling of the decadence of Nineveh and Tyre that he was driven to pray, "Judge of the Nations, spare us yet, / Lest we forget, lest we forget!"

Venice in its decline, Ruskin thought, had clearly forgotten. Renaissance paganism had mingled more and more with its earlier Christian commitment until an unabashed prideful satisfaction with material things had quite superseded all sense of a moral imperative. Venetian society had accordingly passed from strong maturity to decadence, and its decay had reached beyond the Alps to all of western Europe. The "darkness of heart" of nineteenth-century man could be traced to his want of belief and purpose (those who were still sanguine and determined, like the merchants of Bradford, had obviously adopted a false creed). Without an inspiriting faith a culture grew tired and listless. "On the whole," said Ruskin, "these are much *sadder* ages than the early ones; not sadder in a noble and deep way, but in a dim wearied way,—the way of ennui, and jaded intellect, and uncomfortableness of soul and body. The middle ages had their wars and agonies, but also intense delights. Their gold was dashed with blood; but ours is sprinkled with dust. Their life was inwoven with white and purple; ours is one seamless stuff of brown."[26]

Pater's Marius ascribed the comparable sadness of imperial Rome in part to the studied indifference of the Stoics, the inability of Marcus Aurelius himself to cope with the problem of evil in the world or to find a principle of compassion that might alleviate human suffering. And any late Victorian intellectual might have pointed to a systematic philosophic pessimism as a reflection, if not a source, of nineteenth-century disenchantment. James Thomson's nightmared "City" drew on the thought of Leopardi. Hardy's later novels and much of his verse owed a dark debt to Schopenhauer and Hartmann. And John Davidson's manic Testaments derived more than a little from the iconoclasm of Nietzsche.[27] By the nineties a sober academic philosopher could complain that "the recurring wail of isolated melancholy [had] swelled into an inharmoniously harmonious symphony of despair" and pessimism had become the most self-assured of modern philosophies.[28] Thirty years later Albert Schweitzer, convinced that the modern world was in a state of full decadence, blamed that condition on the failure of philosophy to declare and defend ideals by which men might live: "The abdication of thought has been . . . the decisive factor in the collapse of our civilization."[29]

Among the thinkers who abdicated was Oswald Spengler, the exponent of a willful irrationalism which Schweitzer deplored. Spengler's *Decline of the West*, clearly one of the key works of the nineteen twenties, prefigured the belligerent intuitive illogic of the fascists of the thirties and especially the Nazi faith in an ineluctable ruthless destiny operating throughout the historical process. But the book is important for our present purposes only as a recapitulation of concepts of decadence current in the nineteenth century. Though hostile in general to Darwinism and in particular to the notion of evolutionary progress, Spengler described his method as morphological and freely exploited a metaphor from biology: each culture was an organism growing, maturing, and decaying. To illustrate this pattern of development, he invoked a seasonal symbolism, such as Tennyson had used in *Idylls of the King*, but unlike Tennyson he assumed the necessity of the cycle; the summer of a society's growth anticipated the autumn of its decline. Western Europe, he thought (and Ruskin and Morris would have agreed), had known its vital springtime in the "Faustian" culture of the middle ages. Summer had come with the Reformation, and autumn, in the age of Kant and Goethe. Then the nineteenth century had begun the long winter of the West, a period marked by the dominance of science, the appeal to utility, the dearth of metaphysical thinking, the worship of money, and the urbanizing of life in the monstrous megalopolis. True culture was inner, spiritual, and creative, whereas "megalopolitan civilization" was extroverted, materialistic, and imitative, an "existence without inner form." In the civilized winter of the modern world religion had lost its force; art had become arbitrary, experimental, and stylistically uncertain; and the language of educated discourse had all but disappeared.[30]

Spengler's concept of inescapable cultural decadence was actually as vulnerable as the older assumption of unlimited progress. Even if his organic metaphor could adequately suggest the course of ancient empires, no great culture of the nineteenth or twentieth century had operated on an independent cycle; each, in an age of increasingly rapid transport and communication, was subject to the influence of any or all of the others; the dying West might be revitalized by the spiritual East, or both might make a common adjustment to new international conditions. Nonetheless, the notion of decline seemed to have a particular cogency after the First World War when a sense of defeat haunted the victors no less than the vanquished; and Spengler's mood was shared by many who knew nothing of his theory. During the time of battle, D. H. Lawrence spoke bitterly of going off to wait for the new life in America, for England, he said, had still "a long and awful process of corruption and death to go through," whereas America had already "dry-rotted to a point where the final *seed* of the new [was] almost left ready to sprout." Afterwards he saw no object of faith or hope left to society, and he pitied the young who had nothing to affirm: "It's rather hard lines, really, they *inherited* unbelief: like children who expected to be left rich, when their parents died, and find themselves paupers."[31] Likewise, Hardy, nearing the end of his long career, prefaced his *Late Lyrics* with the lament that "we seem threatened with a new Dark Age," a catastrophe to be traced perhaps "to the barbarizing of taste in the younger minds by the dark madness of the late war, the unabashed cultivation of selfishness in all classes, the plethoric growth of knowledge simultaneously with the stunting of wisdom. . . ."[32] Meanwhile, the new English novelists, especially Virginia Woolf and Aldous Huxley, sought the materials of beauty or of irony in a social order they assumed to be futile and decadent. If twentieth-century science constantly reasserted a belief in its own progress, much of the best twentieth-century art, both literature and painting, was committed to negation and despair.

Though the Second World War imposed on England a desperate and often heroic struggle for survival, its aftermath deepened rather than dispelled the sense of imminent decadence. Thus, in his autobiography of 1948, Sir Osbert Sitwell could take leave of the reader with apocalyptic aplomb as "a Citizen of the Sunset Age, an Englishman, who saw the world's great darkness gathering, . . . in a day when the light flared up before it failed."[33] Six years later Wyndham Lewis—to cite an extreme dissident—claimed to see a decline in everything since 1900, "when the supreme and ultimate rot began": "We seem to be running down, everywhere in life, to a final end to all good things; . . . everything . . . is inferior, and there is every reason to suppose that it will get more so, decade by decade"; food, cloth, bricks, furniture, scissors, paper, surgical gut—nothing was as good as it used to be; the "demon of progress" had betrayed the whole of civilization.[34] More recently still, Sir Herbert Read, a man by temperament far more serene and confident than Lewis, remarked that he had persisted "in a simple faith in the natural goodness of man" until he found that faith "certainly no longer tenable," for "the death wish that was once an intellectual fiction has now become a hideous reality and mankind drifts indifferently

to self-destruction. To arrest that drift is beyond our individual capacities; to establish one's individuality is perhaps the only possible protest."[35] Such sentiments, though
emphatic, are broadly representative of an attitude adopted
without much demur by most artists and intellectuals in
our time. Whether or not it raises the occasional unavailing
protest of individuality, the twentieth century has learned
to live with the idea of a present decadence. And its visions
of the future no longer evoke the bucolic utopia of *News
from Nowhere* or the humanized technology of Bellamy's
Looking Backward,[36] but instead the grotesque perspectives
of a *Brave New World* or, more gravely, the hideous statist
nightmare of a *Nineteen Eighty-four*, or, bleakest of all,
the gritty atomism of a Beckett apocalypse.

Though known in his lifetime mainly as the prophet of
science and progress dreaming on the shape of things to
come, H. G. Wells was troubled at intervals from the beginning to the end of his literary career by a darker view
of human prospects; and since his work spans the long
period from the early nineties to the postwar nineteen
forties, his commentary on decadence supplies an unexpected link between the late Victorians and the children
of another lost generation. His first memorable book, *The
Time Machine*, not only described the remote death of all
life on earth, when, in accordance with the second law of
thermodynamics, all useful energy would be dissipated; it
also depicted a less distant age when the intellectual elite,
the Eloi, would be wholly "decadent," the victims of the
"automatic civilization" they had devised and of the masses
they had suppressed, the grim moronic Morlocks of the
underground. In "Decadent World," the last chapter of his
Fate of Man, which appeared in 1939, he predicted—without resort to fantasy or allegory—a coming new barbarism

to differ from the old Dark Ages in "its greater powers of terror, urgency and destruction, and . . . its greater rapidity of wastage."[37] And by the time of his death in 1946 his disillusion was complete; in *Mind at the End of its Tether*— his last work, a brief bitter legacy—he announced: "The end of everything we call life is close at hand and cannot be evaded. . . . There is no way out or round or through the impasse. It is the end. . . . There are thousands of mean, perverted, malicious, heedless and cruel individuals coming into daylight every day, resolute to frustrate the kindlier purposes of man." For there is, he declared, a great hostile force in the universe: the Antagonist, who has willed man's annihilation, with the result "that the human story has already come to an end . . . and that *Homo sapiens,* as he has been pleased to call himself, in his present form, is played out." We have been reduced to the status of futile ants, and "our doomed formicary is helpless as the implacable Antagonist kicks or tramples our world to pieces."[38]

Tono-Bungay of 1908, Wells's best novel and the finest work of his maturity, is less abstract than *The Time Machine* and far less hysterical than the late essays; yet it is no less deeply concerned with the theme of decadence. George Ponderevo, the hero and narrator, whose experience reflects much of Wells's own, must search for values in a world which knows no purpose beyond self-interest. The landed gentry whom his mother serves is moribund, and the great house Bladesover basks in the yellow light of autumn: "The hand of change rests on it all, unfelt, unseen; resting for a while, as it were half reluctantly, before it grips and ends the thing for ever." Yet London seems scarcely more vital: "A city of Bladesovers, the capital of a kingdom of Bladesovers, all much shaken and many altogether in decay, parasitically occupied, insidiously replaced

by alien, unsympathetic and irresponsible elements;—and
withal ruling an adventitious and miscellaneous empire of
a quarter of this daedal earth." Uncle Teddy's rise and fall
as a Napoleon of speculation suggests the course of the
whole society deluding itself with notions of unbounded
progress: "It seems to me indeed at times that all this present commercial civilisation is no more than my poor uncle's
career writ large, a swelling, thinning bubble of assurances;
. . . that it all drifts on perhaps to some tremendous parallel
to his individual disaster." And the radioactive "quap,"
with which George has hoped vainly to recoup Uncle
Teddy's fortunes, becomes a symbol of "atomic decay"
throughout nature, "the ultimate eating-away and dry-rot-
ting and dispersal of all our world." But, apart from this
final horror, which is not to be thought of, immediate social
decadence so obsesses George at the last that he believes
he might better have called his story *Waste* (a title, in-
cidentally, pre-empted the year before *Tono-Bungay* by
Harley Granville-Barker for a social drama of considerable
power.)[39] Wells himself considered calling the novel *The
End of an Age* or *A Picture of the World* or *One Man's
View of England;* but whatever the name, the sense of
doom bulks large, the picture is dark, and the view disen-
chanted. George in the end leaves England to the gathering
night as he makes for the open sea aboard his destroyer,
which represents, he says, the only reality he has found, the
hard clean truth of science. The conviction of decadence
could scarcely be more uncompromising.

*   *   *

But *Tono-Bungay*, though a novel of decadence, is not a
Decadent novel; and Wells, with all his misgivings, is not

to be associated at any stage of his career with the movement known to literary history as the Decadence. We must distinguish between a sense of the reality or possibility of cultural decline, which, as we have seen, has been common among artists and intellectuals for the past century, and an aesthetic mode or temper most apparent, in England, in some of the fiction, minor poetry, and graphic art of the eighteen nineties. The writer concerned with decadence may—like Tennyson and Arnold and Morris and Wells— deplore the direction his society has taken and strive to suggest the values and saving graces it has deserted. The Decadent writer, on the other hand, will display, either in his style or subject matter or in both, his sense of exile from the body politic and his indifference to its fate, or the extent to which a general decay of principles has destroyed his own resolve and positive emotion, or even the degree to which he can experience what Walter Pater called "the fascination of corruption."[40]

It is by no means certain that a decadent age (if any period can be properly so identified) must produce a decadent art. Indeed Rémy de Gourmont, the foremost French theorist of *décadence*, argued that it might on the contrary be "nearer the truth to say that political decadence is the condition most favorable for intellectual flowering."[41] And Ruskin, too, could insist that great art of the past had arisen from dying cultures. "At the moment," he wrote, "when, in any kingdom, you point to the triumphs of its greatest artists, you point also to the determined hour of the kingdom's decline. The names of great painters are like passing bells."[42] In other moods, however, Ruskin declared no less emphatically that the good art was necessarily the product of the good society. And Sir Herbert Read has recently suggested that a decadent culture can lead only to art's

eclipse: "When a civilization is stricken, we shall then no-
tice, along with a declining birth-rate and an increasing
debt, first the censure of originality in art and then art's
complete subservience and defeat."[43] Yet in 1857, on the
first appearance of *Les Fleurs du Mal*, Barbey d'Aurevilly
spoke of Baudelaire as a Decadent writer in a decadent
age;[44] and Baudelaire, whose originality was surely cen-
sured, was in no sense then or ever a servile poet. Nor
were the others in France and England who accepted the
label "Decadent" notably subservient to a middle-class
public; most remained, like Baudelaire, self-consciously beyond the pale of the bourgeois respectabilities. And the
middle classes for their part did not recognize the lives and
works of the Decadents as a sincere or necessary response
to the times, which in many respects still seemed quite
"progressive." On the death of Ernest Dowson in 1900,
Andrew Lang expressed a typically Philistine reaction to
the whole Decadent movement: "By kicking holes in his
boots, crushing in his hat, and avoiding soap, any young
man may achieve a comfortable degree of sordidness, and
then, if his verses are immaterial, and his life suicidal, he
may regard himself as a decadent indeed."[45] But the epithet
"decadent" is ambiguous and confusing. To Lang it con-
noted an aesthetic inferiority and a merely inconsequential
defiance of established convention. To Verlaine and Mallarmé, who were known as *les décadents*, and to Dowson
and Arthur Symons, who are said to have approximated the
French by calling themselves "Dickey-dongs," the term
conveyed no judgment of value; it served simply to describe the art, often painstaking in workmanship, of a late
and highly sophisticated culture.

At Oxford in the eighteen fifties Morris and his friends
all felt that after Tennyson "no farther development was

possible: that we were at the end of all things in poetry."[46] Thirty years later, when Tennyson was still exploiting the resources of language, Pater praised his eclecticism as the necessary modern mode: "How illustrative of monosyllabic effect, of sonorous Latin, of the phraseology of science, of metaphysic, of colloquialism even, are the writings of Tennyson; yet with what a fine, fastidious scholarship throughout!"[47] Tennyson of course was not a Decadent; he had no notion that he might be pushing poetic style to the point of exhaustion,[48] and he did not seek to make his diction a synthesis of the disparate elements of a disintegrating culture. Yet eclecticism is clearly an attribute of literary Decadence, and Pater ascribed it also to Flavian, the gifted selfish young aesthete of *Marius the Epicurean.* Flavian's prose, we are told, was compounded of archaisms and neologies; it was elegant yet racy, precise, calculated, artificial to the extreme, comparable to "the Euphuism of the Elizabethan age and of the modern French romanticists." The Decadent style, particularly in France, that Pater had in mind was, besides, frequently languorous like Pater's own, erudite and elaborate, often bizarre in imagery, sometimes studiously simple, fashioned always, with an unnaturally heightened self-consciousness, as a personal idiom to describe increasingly private reactions and disaffections.

Convinced that his own fleeting experience was for him the one reality in a crumbling world, the Decadent lived wholly in time. External objects had lost their solidity and become, as Pater wrote, simply "impressions," unstable, flickering, inconsistent, which burn and are extinguished with our consciousness of them."[49] The Decadent's work accordingly, even when he sought to mask the self in exotic disguises, was essentially self-expressive. "All artistic

creation," said Oscar Wilde, "is absolutely subjective."[50]
But the subject, the isolated sensibility of the artist, could
scarcely for long evade the burden of withdrawal, the
loneliness, the sense of being abandoned by life, the persis-
tent tedium, and the deep half-understood death-wish.
Though the English Decadents of the nineties had greater
gifts of wit and irony than most of their French counter-
parts (and correspondingly less passionate intensity), a
melancholy defeatism frequently frustrated efforts to establish a comic perspective; and *spleen, ennui, lassitude,* favor-
ite words in French *décadent* vocabulary,[51] became clichés
of English minor poetry. Decadent literature in both coun-
tries was not only urbane but also pre-eminently urban;
but the cities that were its setting were not great centers
of commerce where middle-class men and women went
their monotonous daily rounds; they were rather places of
gas-lit artifice and sinister seduction, offering the jaded appetite every stimulus but no satisfaction, cities of dreadful
night divided between the *haut monde* of ineffable bore-
dom and the dark underworld of forbidden sensations.
Weary of the commonplace and the blandly conventional,
the Decadent might turn in his work to explore or exploit
the strange perversities of sadism, ambiguous sexuality,
neurotic self-injury, all more ominous and alluring when
dimly intimated rather than frankly described. But the
depiction of sin, even in Huysmans' arch-decadent *A Re-
bours,* remained more deliberate and vicarious than con-
vincing; and Dorian Gray's excursions to the opium den
or Arthur Symons' sentimental studies of wronged women
are no more to be taken seriously than Mallarmé's absurd
boast, "*J'ai aimé tout ce qui se résumait en ce mot: chute.*"[52]
At all events, the Decadents avoided consideration of the
larger evils throughout society to which they might have

traced their own sense of cultural decline. They sought, above all, to escape the problems of the age in an art for art's sake that, at least briefly, could engross their full attention. Their attitude in effect foreshadowed that of a distinguished painter in our own time: "You see, painting has become, all art has become, a game by which man distracts himself."[53]

By playing the game with deft delicacy, a few in the English nineties found that they could avoid the perplexities of abstract thought and the questioning of values. Wilde, who was their too articulate spokesman, explained that "we who are born at the close of this wonderful age, are at once too cultured and too critical, too intellectually subtle and too curious of exquisite pleasures, to accept any speculations about life in exchange for life itself."[54] Quietly confusing the life of art and the art of life, the Decadents set aside speculation and for a little while almost forgot about the troublesome implications of even the idea of decadence.

❧ VI ❧

THE PASSION OF THE PAST

Into my heart an air that kills
From yon far country blows:
What are those blue remembered hills
What spires, what farms are those?
—A. E. Housman

I am not a man who was a boy looking at a tree.
I am a man who remembers being a boy looking
at a tree. It is the difference between time, the
endless row of dead bricks, and time, the retake
and coil.
—William Golding

But only in time can the moment in the rose-garden,
The moment in the arbour where the rain beat,
The moment in the draughty church at smoke-fall
Be remembered; involved with past and future.
Only through time time is conquered.
—T. S. Eliot

ROBERT LOUIS STEVENSON was neither Decadent nor greatly troubled by the idea of decadence. But on his first visit to San Francisco, weary and sick for home, he aligned himself with what seemed to be England's imminent decline; as if affronted by a frontier vitality, he told his American friends,

> You speak another tongue than mine,
>   Though both were English born.
> I toward the night of time decline;
>   You mount into the morn.
>
> Youth shall grow great and strong and free,
>   But age must still decay;
> Tomorrow for the States—for me,
>   England and Yesterday.

Yet the yesterday to which he turned was a span of private rather than public time; though still, as he confessed, "young in years" (he was actually just thirty), he longed to recover his own past, to know again the security and romance of a lost and strangely distant boyhood. Back in England, when he wrote *A Child's Garden of Verses*, he depicted the child as eagerly imagining the attitudes he would assume when "grown to man's estate," proudly conning each part like the "little Actor" of Wordsworth's "Ode." But when, more typically, he spoke from his own maturity, he reversed the perspective; with a gentle sentiment he mourned the vanishing forever of a personal past and the death of another and better self:

> Sing me a song of a lad that is gone,
>   Say, could that lad be I?
> Merry of soul he sailed on a day
>   Over the sea to Skye.
>
> Billow and breeze, islands and seas,
>   Mountains of rain and sun,
> All that was good, all that was fair,
>   All that was me is gone.[1]

With the several literary generations of his century, Stevenson shared a habit of reminiscence. Though, like his peers, he was relatively reticent about his private life, he remained, like them, almost compulsively self-conscious, fascinated by the meaning of his impressions and the possible coherence of his essential being. He may well have believed quite literally that an actual self had gone beyond recall with the sea-going lad. For all things constantly moved and changed in time, and the very cell structure of the physical body was renewed, and so replaced, every few years. If, as Hume had suggested, the self was but the aggregate of its sensations, then no man could be sure of his real identity; each might have as many selves as the points of time at which he chose to appraise his experience.[2] "To such a tremulous wisp," said Pater, "constantly reforming itself on the stream, to a single sharp impression, with a sense in it, a relic more or less fleeting, of such moments gone by, what is real in our life fines itself down."[3]

If, however, as Kant had argued, the self were not merely the sum of its perceptions but rather a factor able to relate, organize, and interpret those perceptions, then a man might discover a continuity and consistency of the self in its passage through time; the boy sailing to Skye might be one with the man at home in remote Samoa. Kant's relating factor was in effect Wordsworth's "natural piety," the force by which the child could be seen to be father of the man and all the days of a life to be bound each to each in a resolved harmony. *The Prelude* was expressly written so that the poet, by a recovery of the past, might achieve such a faith in the integrity of the self as would prepare him to bear the greater burdens of the future:

> my hope has been, that I might fetch
> Invigorating thoughts from former years:
> Might fix the wavering balance of my mind,
> And haply meet reproaches too, whose power
> May spur me on, in manhood now mature
> To honourable toil.

For every past victory was a measure of the soul's potential:

> So feeling comes in aid
> Of feeling, and diversity of strength
> Attends us, if but once we have been strong.[4]

If the present seemed wavering and amorphous, the past at least was fixed and definite. Natural piety involved an honesty of memory willing to confront the quite immutable truth of antecedents. Accordingly, Maggie Tulliver in *The Mill on the Floss*, who has once been strong, refuses to yield to a last temptation "when the sense of contradiction with her past self in her moments of strength and clearness" comes upon her "like a pang of conscious degradation." And even the criminal Magwitch of *Great Expectations*, most of whose "time" was sadly misspent, at length reaches reverence of a sort for the accomplished fact; when dying, he never once, we are told, "tried to bend the past out of its eternal shape."[5] More sensitive men than Magwitch sought, like Wordsworth or like Maggie, to place the changeful self in the perspective of its origins and accordingly to realize a sense of stability in a turning world and, at best, the imperturbable strength of acceptance:

> How strange, that all
> The terrors, pains, and early miseries,
> Regrets, vexations, lassitudes interfused
> Within my mind, should e'er have borne a part,
> And that a needful part, in making up
> The calm existence that is mine when I
> Am worthy of myself.[6]

The nineteenth century was accordingly the great age of English autobiography. Completing the first draft of *The Prelude* in 1805, Wordsworth declared it "a thing unprecedented in literary history that a man should talk so much about himself."[7] Yet before long other Romantics were quite as eager to discover themselves in past time. Coleridge, though he digressed constantly and brilliantly from the subject, designed his major prose work, the great amorphous *Biographia Literaria*, as "Biographical Sketches of my Literary Life and Opinions." Byron shaped his masterpiece, *Don Juan*, not only to carry his running commentary on modern life in general but also to provide a full, though ironic, perspective on his own education and experience, his memories of Newstead Abbey and his mixed feelings for the England he had loved and hated. Hazlitt, twenty-five years after the event, recalled the circumstances of his first acquaintance with the poets and the very dialogues that had first awakened his understanding from a "dumb and brutish" sleep. And De Quincey realized his best talents in the compulsion to remember fact and dream with preternatural vividness, as in "The English Mail-Coach," or to seek the source of present nightmares in past horrors —as in the *Opium-Eater* and *Suspiria de Profundis*—and so to find "years that were far asunder . . . bound together by subtle links of suffering derived from a common root."[8]

Throughout the Victorian period the autobiographical impulse flourished more variously than ever before. The keeping of journals and diaries as memorials to the immediate past, a practice already brought to a considerable perfection by the Romantics, became a common pursuit, to some indeed almost a responsibility, an occasion for self-accounting and communion. But there were also many less fragmentary memoirs and career books, some as earnest as Mrs. Oliphant's life story or Frederic Harrison's,[9] a few as egregiously self-satisfied as W. P. Frith's reminiscences or as flagrantly exhibitionistic as George Moore's unlikely *Confessions of a Young Man*. Trollope, who wrote the most businesslike and one of the most engaging of such volumes, concluded—after a statement of his total earnings from his publications—with a characteristic disclaimer: "It will not, I trust, be supposed by any reader that I have intended in this so-called autobiography to give a record of my inner life. No man ever did so truly,—and no man ever will."[10] Nonetheless, as John Morley pointed out in his own matter-of-fact *Recollections*, anyone who looks closely into that "other world we call the Past" should expect to "stumble on plenty of material for self-surprise and self-reproof."[11] And the quality of the inner life to be recovered by deliberate self-examination and sometimes self-reproof was a central concern in many Victorian autobiographies, ranging from Ruskin's *Praeterita* and Newman's *Apologia* and the "mental history" of John Stuart Mill, to less candid revelations such as Oscar Wilde's *De Profundis*, which sentimentalized the role that the fallen ego might have played, or Richard Jefferies' *Story of My Heart*, the spiritual adventure of one who proclaimed too stridently his faith in fleshly perfection. Autobiography appeared openly or with varying degrees of obliquity in countless Victorian poems —in *Modern Love* and *The Unknown Eros*, in *The House of Life* and *In Memoriam*, in Arnold's lyrics to Marguerite and Hopkins's "terrible" sonnets, in Swinburne's allegorical *Thalassius* and Henley's journalistic *In Hospital*. It lurked behind the prose ironies of *Sartor Resartus* and concealed itself in Pater's *Imaginary Portraits* and "The Child in the House." And for the first time in English fiction it provided the novelist a major source of theme and content. Especially in the *Bildungsroman*, the novel of a young man's growth and initiation, the subjective element bulked large; David Copperfield, Arthur Pendennis, Richard Feverel, Ernest Pontifex, Pater's Marius, Jude Fawley—each of these reflected to a degree his creator's need to see a meaning in the personal past, to find the true self in time. The fact that the ending of the typical *Bildungsroman* was aesthetically inconclusive was evidence simply that the novelist, whose own development was still in process, could not detach himself sufficiently from his protagonist to pass a disinterested final judgment on the success or failure of his orientation.

Detachment, however, was a prime objective in much of the autobiographical writing. Thackeray suggested how the aim might be achieved in fiction: his Henry Esmond, anticipating Henry Adams by many years, tells his own story in the third person; Esmond calls himself, as the stages of his growth dictate, the boy, the lad, young Esmond, Mr. Esmond, the Captain, the Colonel, as if the past selves were quite distinct and the identity between them had to be established.[12] Meredith similarly employed the device of the third person in *Modern Love*, where the poet-narrator at the beginning and the end regards his other self, the speaker throughout the body of the sequence, as an altogether different man, a comedian moving blindly through a tragedy of egoism, "Condemned to do the flitting of the bat." And Newman invoked the same means of distancing the record, in the title of his great self-defense, *Apologia pro Vita Sua*—not, we observe, *pro Vita Mea*— "Being a History of his Religious Opinions." Nonetheless, like most of the prose autobiographies, the book itself was written in the first person; and Newman had to find subtler ways of attaining objectivity—through the precision of language, the quiet persuasiveness of tone, and the avoidance of irrelevant emotional commentary. "It is not at all pleasant," he confessed in his preface, "for me to be egotistical; nor to be criticized for being so. It is not pleasant to reveal to high and low, young and old, what has gone on within me from my early years."[13] Darwin, writing with less misgiving (since his audience was to be his own children and grandchildren), found detachment by assuming a perspective beyond mortal time: "I have attempted," he said, "to write the following account of myself, as if I were a dead man in another world looking back at my own life. Nor have I found this difficult, for life is nearly over with me."[14] And Mill, convinced that few could be much concerned with his uneventful career, suggested with complete dispassion that "in an age of transition in opinions" there might still possibly be "somewhat both of interest and of benefit in noting the successive phases of any mind which was always pressing forward, equally ready to learn and to unlearn either from its own thoughts or from those of others."[15]

Like Wordsworth, who in *The Prelude* made no direct allusion at all to the passionate affair with Annette Vallon, in which psychological critics now see a portentous significance, the major Victorian autobiographers selected at will from their pasts without obvious self-repression or loss of real perspective. Newman, for whatever reason, excluded his home life as a child from the history of his religious opinions; and Mill, though much preoccupied with his father's character and ideas of education, found no need in his *Autobiography* to honor his mother or even indeed to acknowledge her existence.[16] Ruskin, on the other hand, recovered his childhood with a vividness reminiscent of the opening pages of *David Copperfield*, and for his edification and ours re-established both his formidable parents as "visi-

ble powers of nature." With an intense self-consciousness
and a great power of self-effacement, he moved back in
Praeterita almost to his birth, or at least to the earliest home
he could remember: "I write these few prefatory words on
my father's birthday, in what was once my nursery in his
old house,—to which he brought my mother and me, sixty-
two years since, I being then four years old." Yet, despite
the brilliance of his analysis, he felt no necessity to recall
the unhappiness of his unnatural marriage. "I have written,
. . ." he explained, "frankly, garrulously, and at ease; speaking, of what it gives me joy to remember, at any length I
like—sometimes very carefully of what I think it may be
useful for others to know; and passing in total silence
things which I have no pleasure in reviewing, and which
the reader would find no help in the account of."[17]

Yet the fact that Ruskin and the others chose not to review unpleasant or unduly intimate detail did not of course
mean that they had forgotten any essential part of their
experience. Hazlitt, to be sure, complained that most of
the past as lived by the individual was no longer effective,
for "even in our prime the strongest impressions leave . . .
little traces of themselves behind, and the last object is
driven out by the succeeding one."[18] But De Quincey was
closer to the broad assumptions of the nineteenth century
when he insisted: "Of this, at least, I feel assured, that there
is no such thing as *forgetting* possible to the mind; a thousand accidents may and will interpose a veil between our
present consciousness and the secret inscriptions on the
mind; accidents of the same sort will also rend away this
veil; but alike, whether veiled or unveiled, the inscription
remains for ever; just as the stars seem to withdraw before
the common light of day, whereas, in fact, we all know
that it is the light which is drawn over them as a veil—and

that they are waiting to be revealed, when the obscuring daylight shall have withdrawn."[19] Wordsworth believed in the sanctity and sometimes the terror of memory and in the high importance of his own remembering. And Ruskin, however great his will to suppress painful recollection, considered man's capacity for recall virtually unlimited, and strong enough, at least in creative men, almost to revive the intense physicality of the powerful sense impression. Turner, he said, observed even the most transient natural detail and treasured it up for future use; "there was not one of the things which he wished to represent that stayed for so much as five seconds together: but none of them escaped for all that: they are sealed up in that strange storehouse of his; he may take one of them out, perhaps, this day twenty years, and paint it in his dark room, far away."[20] Later in the Victorian period Samuel Butler declared memory the definitive attribute of life itself; the very amoeba, he insisted, remembers experiences in past generations, and all life is "the being possessed of a memory —the life of a thing at any moment is the memories which at that moment it retains."[21] The whole past accordingly, though buried in unconscious depths, remained always to help shape every man's present, and no event or impression in all of human time could be wilfully dismissed or expunged.

Convinced of some such truth, Pater's Marius, we are told, remained essentially "of the poetic temper: by which, I mean," Pater explained, "among other things, that quite independently of that pensive age he lived much, and as it were by system, in reminiscence." Marius must therefore judge every sensation of the present in the light of one question: "How will it look to me, and what shall I value it, this day next year?"—for "in any given day or month

one's main concern was its impression for the memory."
And when his friend the aesthetic Flavian dies, he must
linger for an unconscionable time, "standing by the dead,
watching, with deliberate purpose to fix in his memory
every detail, that he might have this picture in reserve,
should any hour of forgetfulness hereafter come to him
with the temptation to feel completely happy again. . . .
From mere tenderness of soul he would not forget one
circumstance in all that; as a man might piously stamp on
his memory the death-scene of a brother wrongfully condemned to die, against a time that may come."[22] If the active Victorian could say with Tennyson's Ulysses, "I am a
part of all that I have met" (that is, I have left my mark
everywhere on the great world outside), the reflective man
could feel with Marius, in effect: All that I have met is a
part of me—I am today what I have assimilated of the past;
I am inescapably the creature of memory.

In much nineteenth-century literature the past remembered proved matter for remorse or self-recrimination or
simply bitterness. The guilty secret, particularly of the
woman "with a past," was part of the stock-in-trade of the
Victorian melodrama and the sensational novel; and on occasion in more serious fiction, as in the Bulstrode story of
Middlemarch, the burden of concealed sin became the subject of a trenchant analysis. In some of his early verse
Thomas Hardy anticipated the acerbity of his later prose;
the disillusioned lover of "Neutral Tones," bruised by sub-
sequent experience, remembers every bleak detail of an
estrangement years before:

> Since then, keen lessons that love deceives,
> And wrings with wrong, have shaped to me
> Your face, and the God-curst sun, and a tree,
> And a pond edged with grayish leaves.

Dickens scarcely disguised his own traumatic memories of the blacking warehouse in the Strand when he allowed David Copperfield to recall the horrors of Murdstone and Grinby's:

> The deep remembrance of the sense I had, of being utterly without hope now; of the shame I felt in my position; of the misery it was to my young heart to believe that day by day what I had learned, and thought, and delighted in, and raised my fancy and my emulation up by, would pass away from me, little by little, never to be brought back any more; cannot be written.[23]

Christina Rossetti, on the other hand, full of self-reproach, regretted with a sad conscience every missed opportunity for love and service. And her brother Dante Gabriel with some deep personal urgency registered the sense of wasted time, the wrong done to the spirit by lethargy and procrastination; one of the strongest sonnets in *The House of Life* casts about to find images adequate to picture "the lost days of my life until to-day" and then concludes dramatically:

> I do not see them here; but after death
>   God knows I know the faces I shall see,
> Each one a murdered self, with low last breath.
>   "I am thyself,—what hast thou done to me?"
> "And I—and I—thyself," (lo! each one saith,)
>   "And thou thyself to all eternity!"

But, if misgivings about the private past were not uncommon, the usual Victorian response was far more positive. George Meredith, describing the first love of Richard Feverel and Lucy, reflected what "mere sparks" our highest moments really are and yet "how in the distance of time they revive, and extend, and glow, and make us think them full the half, and the best of the fire, of our lives!"[24] In an age of great changes and large uncertainties many clung to

the memory of "lost days" that they could admire or idealize or often quite unabashedly sentimentalize. William
Allingham, for example, sang nostalgically of innocent impressions:

> Four ducks on a pond,
> A grass-bank beyond,
> A blue sky of spring,
> White clouds on the wing;
> What a little thing
> To remember for years—
> To remember with tears![25]

And Burne-Jones long after the event cherished the memory of a wonderful Pre-Raphaelite menage in Red Lion
Square and an unreal magical 1856, "a year in which I
think it never rained, nor clouded, but was blue summer
from Christmas to Christmas, and London streets glittered,
and it was always morning, and the air sweet and full of
bells."[26] The good time past was deliberately evoked not
only by mementos in wood and paper, glass and brass, the
tangible souvenirs of which the Victorians were inordi-
nately fond, but also by returns to scenes hallowed by association. Thus Tennyson, as *In Memoriam* suggests, eager
to come to terms with life and death, revisited the reverend
walls of Cambridge, which his dead friend had once filled
with "rapt oration." Or, again, much later, as a short lyric
recounts, he sought out the valley of Cauteretz in the
Pyrenees where he had walked with Hallam more than
thirty years earlier, and the persistence of the landscape
now recovered the past, for the river's

> living voice to me was as the voice of the dead,
> And all along the valley, by rock and cave and tree,
> The voice of the dead was a living voice to me.

Memory of a lost emotion might recall all the vividness of the sense impressions that accompanied it, as the husband's recollection, in *Modern Love*, of a protective embrace assumes a fresh physical immediacy:

> Well knew we that Life's greatest treasure lay
> With us, and of it was our talk. "Ah, yes!
> Love dies!" I said: I never thought it less.
> She yearned to me that sentence to unsay.
> Then when the fire domed blackening, I found
> Her cheek was salt against my kiss, and swift
> Up the sharp scale of sobs her breast did lift:—
> Now am I haunted by that taste! that sound!

Or, conversely, the sharp sensation, like the roar of the mountain stream, might evoke past emotions. Wordsworth, who more than anyone else established for the Victorians the sanctity of memory, left striking examples of this mode of recall; the song of the cuckoo, bringing back "visionary hours," helped beget for him once again the "golden time" of boyhood, and the sight of a tree or a single field or the "Pansy at my feet" spoke to him sadly of something that was gone. In a suppressed early "Song" Tennyson asked,

> Who can tell
> Why to smell
> The violet, recalls the dewy prime
> Of Youth and buried time?

And—though less bluntly—he allowed the dreamer of "A Dream of Fair Women" to make like associations with the same odor:

> The smell of violets, hidden in the green,
>   Pour'd back into my empty soul and frame
> The times when I remember to have been
>   Joyful and free from blame.

Similarly Hardy in one of his rhymed dialogues made the shock of cold water the sensation by which an aging woman relives for the moment a happier past, a lovers' meeting by a waterfall:

> "Whenever I plunge my arm, like this,
> In a basin of water, I never miss
> The sharp sweet sense of a fugitive day
> Fetched back from its thickening shroud of gray. . . ."[27]

In prose fiction, Dickens was best able to endow the concrete sensuous detail with heightened particularity and symbolic significance; and especially in *David Copperfield*, which is above all the others his novel of memory, he found frequent use for the intense impression as a bridge between present and past. Long after Dora's death, the scent of a geranium leaf strikes David "with a half comical, half serious wonder as to what change has come over [him] in a moment" until he sees once more an enchanted greenhouse and Dora's straw hat, ribbons, and curls against the blossoms. Or, again, when David returns at last to Agnes, he relives the mood in which he once mused about other wanderers:

The feeling with which I used to watch the tramps, as they came into the town on those wet evenings, at dusk, and limped past, with their bundles drooping over their shoulders at the ends of sticks, came freshly back to me; fraught, as then, with the smell of damp earth, and wet leaves and briar, and the sensation of the very airs that blew upon me in my own toilsome journey.[28]

So, quietly, without conscious effort, David achieves the sort of recovery of the past that Proust's hero seeks with great deliberation.

The recurrence of sense impressions frequently brought with it a sense of *déjà vu*, that is, of having already encountered in some hidden past a present situation. Appropriately enough, David Copperfield digresses on the common illusion: "We have all some experience of a feeling, that comes over us occasionally, of what we are saying and doing having been said and done before, in a remote time—of our having been surrounded, dim ages ago, by the same faces, objects, and circumstances—of our knowing perfectly well what will be said next, as if we suddenly remembered it!"[29] But neither David nor Dickens himself seems to have attached a metaphysical meaning to the experience. Rossetti, on the other hand, saw in it possible intimations of immortality, the token of love's transcendence; his lyric "Sudden Light" is the clearest Victorian expression of the *déjà vu,* and the most eloquent:

> I have been here before,
>   But when or how I cannot tell,
> I know the grass beyond the door,
>   The sweet keen smell,
> The sighing sound, the lights around the shore.
>
> You have been mine before—
>   How long ago I may not know;
> But just when at that swallow's soar
>   Your neck turned so,
> Some veil did fall—I knew it all of yore.

Then from the very intensity of the impressions, the ultimate graphic pattern—as if the moment had existed always in some ideal world—there comes an argument for the eternal return of life and love:

> Has this been thus before?
> And shall not thus time's eddying flight
> Still with our lives our loves restore
>   In death's despite,
> And day and night yield one delight once more?

Rossetti's question anticipates Browning's in the late lyric "Never the Time and the Place," where the mild spring weather has awakened memories of the loved one:

> Do I hold the Past
> Thus firm and fast
> Yet doubt if the Future hold I can?
> This path so soft to pace shall lead
> Through the magic of May to herself indeed!

But the question here is purely rhetorical; Browning affirms at once his confidence that the fixity of the past is the clear warrant of continuity. Tennyson, on the other hand, like Rossetti was haunted by the mysteries of time, and much of his most characteristic work explored the psychology of nostalgia. "Tears, Idle Tears" defines in vivid imagery a nameless grief risen "from the depth of some divine despair," on "thinking of the days that are no more," and seeks to convey, as the poet explained in a prose gloss, "the passion of the past, the abiding in the transient," and a "sort of mystic, *dämonisch* feeling."[30] *In Memoriam*, after a poignant review of the past shared with Hallam, reaches its climax in the great ninety-fifth lyric, where the poet alone on a stilled summer night reads the dead man's letters:

> And strangely on the silence broke
>   The silent-speaking words, and strange
>   Was love's dumb cry defying change
> To test his worth; and strangely spoke

The faith, the vigour, bold to dwell
  On doubts that drive the coward back,
  And keen thro' wordy snares to track
Suggestion to her inmost cell.

So word by word, and line by line,
  The dead man touch'd me from the past,
  And all at once it seem'd at last
The living soul was flash'd on mine,

And mine in this was wound, and whirl'd
  About empyreal heights of thought
  And came on that which is, and caught
The deep pulsations of the world,

Aeonian music measuring out
  The steps of Time—the shocks of Chance—
  The blows of Death . . .

So presented, the experience partakes of mystical revelation; the past briefly recovered leads to a dazzling vision of "that which is," a state of absolute being beyond the reach of death and chance and time itself. At intervals throughout his life Tennyson apparently knew moments when "The mortal limit of the Self was loosed," and the prelude to such transcendence seems always to have been, as "The Ancient Sage" suggests, the troubling sense of the past—even in boyhood when the child could have little personal past to remember:

        "for oft
On me, when boy, there came what then I call'd,
Who knew no books and no philosophies,
In my boy-phrase, 'The Passion of the Past.'
The first gray streak of earliest summer-dawn,
The last long stripe of waning crimson gloom,

As if the late and early were but one—
A height, a broken grange, a grove, a flower
Had murmurs, 'Lost and gone, and lost and gone!'
A breath, a whisper—some divine farewell—
Desolate sweetness—far and far away—
What had he loved, what had he lost, the boy?
I know not, and I speak of what has been."

Though this passage with its hinting at a pre-existence recalls Wordsworth's "Intimations" ode, the boy in Tennyson has little of the Wordsworthian child's unself-conscious
satisfaction with his environment; already he feels a sense
of dislocation in the present, an adult hunger for a remote
elusive past.

Few other Victorians expressed their emotion in terms
so "mystical," but many felt a deep nostalgia, a yearning
for the "far country" of *A Shropshire Lad*—

That is the land of lost content,
I see it shining plain,
The happy highways where I went
And cannot come again.

Recent biographers and critics have sometimes been too
ready to identify images and symbols as expressing or con-
cealing a desire to return to the womb; but the longing for
a lost Eden and, more generally, the whole cult of childhood in nineteenth-century literature often do seem to in-
vite a psychological interpretation. The fantasies of Lewis
Carroll and George Macdonald, especially, seem in many
details to require such analysis. William Empson has remarked that "to make the dream-story from which *Wonderland* was elaborated seem Freudian one has only to tell
it."[31] And Robert L. Wolff has skillfully cast both Freud-

ian and Jungian lights and shadows across Macdonald's
strange fairy tales.[32] But in other works where the symbolism was less obvious, the return to the child's world
could signify, as in *Marius the Epicurean*, simply the
adult's effort to make his peace with the past and so to
come to terms with his present self. Shortly before his
death Marius returns to White Nights, his long-deserted
family home. There, as he tends the neglected graves of his
parents, he not only recovers his deep respect for his
mother's serenity and grace but also, and now for the first
time, feels an inexplicable kinship with the father he had
never known and always subconsciously rejected: "And
with that came a blinding rush of kindness, as if two
alienated friends had come to understand each other at
last."[33] Having thus confronted the past with sympathy
and mature acceptance, Marius has achieved a final integration of spirit.

Early in the new century H. G. Wells suggested through
a compelling short story both the spell and the menace of a
nostalgia for a buried time. "The Door in the Wall"—
patently sexual in much of its symbolism and implication—
describes a lonely child's vision of an enchanted garden,
behind a green door in a high white wall, where the in-
truder feels instant joy and "a keen sense of homecoming,"
and where a benevolent somber woman, "very gentle and
grave," shows him a picture book of his own life. Before
opening the door, the boy has had not only the strong desire to do so, but also "the clearest conviction that either
it was unwise or it was wrong of him—he could not tell
which—to yield to this attraction," and he has known instinctively that "his father would be very angry." Afterwards, when his father, who is a lawyer and a grim
rationalist, punishes him for telling lies about the garden,

he succeeds in suppressing the memory. But he can never quite forget, and now and again throughout his career he catches glimpses of the strange familiar door in the wall: once when his eagerness not to be late for school overcomes his wish to stop, once when he cannot afford to let anything interfere with his arrival at Oxford for a fellowship, once when he does not care to keep a lady waiting. Eventually he achieves distinction in politics and is even asked to join the Cabinet; but he is dissatisfied always with his successes and tortured by increasingly frequent thoughts of the bypassed door. In the end his dead body is found at the bottom of a deep excavation; he has apparently wandered through an unlocked gate in the hoarding. It remains a question whether the dream of a lost peace and security has ultimately released him from the distractions of the world or merely betrayed him.[34]

The Victorians, however, in life or in books, were unlikely to be destroyed by the passion of the past. If many could understand Tennyson's longing for the days that were no more, most at the same time acknowledged a responsibility to the present, the commitment of the Tennysonian Arthur to the task at hand—

> seeing that the King must guard
> That which he rules, and is but as the hind
> To whom a space of land is given to plow,
> Who may not wander from the allotted field
> Before his work be done . . .[35]

Macaulay, who tried to find himself in history, told his sister that he had the "power of forgetting what surrounds me, and of living with the past, the future, the distant, and the unreal."[36] But whatever his skill at imagining himself in another time, he made abundantly clear the relevance of the historical record to the nineteenth century, to the milieu of his England and his age. And Macaulay was but typical of a common will to let a contemplation of the past, private no less than public, subserve a more immediate need. Memories of the lad that was gone, the childhood that was and was not, the days enjoyed and the days lost, the vivid sense impression, the far country—all these could help "fix the wavering balance" of one's mind and perhaps act as spurs "to honourable toil," or at least give the brief peremptory moment some semblance of perspective, extension and solidity. The meaning of the past remembered lay in its power to enhance the quality of life in the all-demanding present.

⋅⊰ VII ⊱⋅

THE LIVING PRESENT

> Whatever we may think or affect to think of the
> present age, we cannot get out of it; we must
> suffer with its sufferings, and enjoy with its en-
> joyments; we must share in its lot, and, to be
> either useful or at ease, we must even partake its
> character. No man whose good qualities were
> mainly those of another age, ever had much influ-
> ence on his own.
>
> –John Stuart Mill

However seductive it may have appeared in retrospect, the past, whether private or public, receded more
and more rapidly as the tempo of nineteenth-century
change and innovation accelerated. When, as Hardy put it,
the Victorians "looked closelier at Time," they saw only

> his ghostly arms revolving
> To sweep off woeful things with prime,
> Things sinister with things sublime
> Alike dissolving.[1]

The past persisted, if at all, in mere fragments; its whole-
ness and even its reality became a subjective illusion to be
experienced, briefly and precariously, through the exercise
of the disciplined imagination. "The path we came by,"
said the Tennyson of *In Memoriam,* was already "shadowed
by the growing hour," its perils and charms alike fortu-

116

nately half-hidden, "Lest life should fail in looking back." It was clear that, if life were in any degree to succeed, one must accept its given conditions, the challenge of the imperious present, which, if not wholly to be approved, was at all events to be recognized. After each imagined excursion into another time, one must return resolutely, like Browning's Abt Volger, to the here and now, "the C Major of this life." For here alone was his vantage point, "A place" (in the words of Mrs. Browning) "to stand and love in for a day,/ With darkness and the death-hour rounding it."

Mrs. Browning's own most ambitious work, the verse novel *Aurora Leigh*, was feverishly contemporary; the sole function of the poet, declared Aurora, was "to represent the age, . . . this live, throbbing age,/ That brawls, cheats, maddens, calculates, aspires," for

> To flinch from modern varnish, coat, or flounce,
> Cry out for togas and the picturesque,
> Is fatal,—foolish, too. King Arthur's self
> Was commonplace to Lady Guinevere;
> And Camelot to minstrels seemed as flat
> As Fleet Street to our poets.

Ruskin, though himself always much concerned with history, applauded both the precept and the example; *Aurora Leigh*, he said, was quite simply "the greatest poem in the language, unsurpassed by anything but Shakespeare."[2] And his enthusiasm conditioned his disappointment three years later with the first four *Idylls of the King;* "It seems to me," he told Tennyson, "that so great power ought not to be spent on visions of things past but on the living present."[3] Tennyson could have explained that his themes were essentially relevant to any time and that he had turned to

the Arthurian past not foolishly in search of the picturesque but with deliberate intent to achieve a perspective on
human values and an aesthetic distance from present distractions. Instead, he became uncomfortably self-conscious
when accused of "looking back," of seeking escape from
his own live, throbbing age; and he did not begin concerted
work on the later *Idylls* till ten years after the composition
of the 1859 volume. He had been sensitive to the peremptory demand of the present ever since the writing of his
early "Morte d'Arthur," which he had framed in a Victorian genre piece called "The Epic," suggesting, half in
irony, half in apology, that "perhaps some modern touches
here and there" redeemed the medieval subject matter
"from the charge of nothingness." He had likewise devised
a modern frame for the mock heroics of *The Princess*. And
he had prefaced his retelling of the ancient legend of
Godiva with the remark that he wrote it while waiting
for the train at Coventry, with the avowed purpose of
showing that the social conscience was not a nineteenth-
century invention—

> Not only we, the latest seed of Time,
> New men, that in the flying of a wheel
> Cry down the past, not only we, that
> Prate of rights and wrongs, have loved the people well.

The major poets, however, as Mrs. Browning rather un-
poetically argued, were far less likely to cry down the past
than to denigrate the present. Tennyson and Arnold in
particular were nostalgic for a lost age of faith, responsive
to the appeal of a classical culture, restive in the iron time
of prose and progress. George Eliot, in a late notebook dialogue with herself, commented on the fact that "it is pre-

cisely the most poetic minds that most groan over the vulgarity of the present, its degenerate sensibility to beauty, eagerness for materialistic explanation, noisy triviality." But to this observation she immediately, with cool rationality, added another: "Perhaps they would have had the same complaint to make about the age of Elizabeth, if, living then, they had fixed their attention on its more sordid elements, or had been subject to the grating influence of its everyday meannesses, and had sought refuge from them in the contemplation of whatever suited their taste in a former age."[4] For her own part she confessed to "an inborn beguilement" which carried her "affection and regret continually into an imaginary past"; yet she insisted that she would lose "all sense of moral proportion unless [she kept] alive a stronger attachment to what [was] near, and a power of admiring" what she best knew and understood.[5] Rather than be herself in another age, she would prefer to be another and more vital self in the encompassing present. Hers was the commonsensical bias of the Victorian rationalist, the refusal to idealize the past; if she too yearned for a lost faith, she could still not delude herself into imagining that past ages were easier or more humane than her own. Much earlier in the period Macaulay, whose aspirations were somewhat less spiritual than George Eliot's, had begun his great *History* with a like conviction: "Those who compare the age on which their lot has fallen with a golden age which exists only in their imagination may talk of degeneracy and decay: but no man who is correctly informed as to the past will be disposed to take a morose or desponding view of the present."[6] Many years later Bertrand Russell, in some respects the last of the late Victorians, could present a short story of a past allegedly

golden but actually so repressed and pharisaical as to rec-
oncile the twentieth-century narrator to his own perilous
time.[7] Life indeed was not to fail in looking back.

Ruskin saw an irony in the fact that the Victorians,
committed in many ways to the idea of progress, were frequently so reactionary in their literary and aesthetic tastes,
so distrustful of innovation. "The furniture and personages
of our romance," he complained, "are sought, when the
writer desires to please most easily, in the centuries which
we profess to have surpassed in everything; the art which
takes us into the present times is considered as both daring
and degraded." The great ages of the past were quite different; they reverenced their ancestors, yet "nevertheless
thought their own deeds and ways of life the fitting subject
for their arts of painting or of verse. . . . The Greeks and
mediaevals honoured, but did not imitate their forefathers;
we imitate, but do not honour."[8] Ruskin himself had both
reverence for the past and an almost overwhelming sense
of obligation to the present. He asked that the experience
of history be respected, not that the practice of another age
be duplicated. He looked back for guidance and perspective rather than for ready-made solutions to present aesthetic and social problems. And despite his charge that the
will to imitate was pervasive, a good many of his contemporaries were in fact no less concerned than he to discover
the immediate relevance of the past. The authors of popular romance might indeed offer an easy escape into freer,
bolder times. But the serious novelists often designed their
historical fiction as oblique or even direct commentary on
the present. Kingsley's *Hypatia*, for example, bore the subtitle "New Foes with an Old Face" as a reminder that the
Victorian reader might recognize amid the schisms of fifth-

century Egypt his "own likeness in toga and tunic, instead of coat and bonnet";[9] Bulwer Lytton's *Last of the Barons* made Warwick, the people's aristocrat, spokesman for a program remarkably like that of the Tory Radicals of Young England in the eighteen forties;[10] *Romola* suggested parallels between Savonarola's Florence and George Eliot's London; and *Weir of Hermiston* carried Stevenson's conviction that the code of a heroic yet savage past had never been wholly outgrown or forgotten.[11] At the beginning of *A Tale of Two Cities*, Dickens wryly described the old regime in France as "so far like the present period, that some of its noisiest authorities insisted on its being received for good or for evil, in the superlative degree of comparison only." His public was thus alerted at the outset not only to the possible analogy between past and present but also to his will to view both with a due sense of proportion.

Dickens, of course, usually found a fitting subject nearer home than the French Revolution; his characteristic work, though vibrant with memories of his own lost childhood, was rooted far less in history than in the realities of a present-day society. And his readers, however much attracted to the furniture of old romance in other writers, were frequently prepared—in literature and in life—to forget the public past altogether and to concentrate attention on their own tumultuous age. Representative titles throughout the period testify to the Victorian absorption in things close and new, or else in old ideas and practices reconstituted to meet present needs: "Signs of the Times" and *Hard Times for These Times*, "The Function of Criticism at the Present Time" and *The Present Position of Catholics in England*, *Modern Painters*, *Modern Love*, and *A Modern Lover*, *The Way We Live Now*, the *Contemporary Review*, the *Nineteenth Century*, *Latter-Day Pamphlets* and "The Spirit of

the Age," the *New Review* and the *New Moral World*,
New Grub Street, The New Republic, "The New Sirens,"
New Arabian Nights, and the *New English Dictionary*.

Such modernity of concern should have pleased Aurora
Leigh. Yet Mrs. Browning herself must have known the
difficulty of enthusiastically exploiting modern materials
without capitulating to what was false or aesthetically alien
in modern values. The poets of the so-called Spasmodic
School, to which *Aurora Leigh* at least should be related,
rushed frenetically at contemporary life only to find its
harshness bruise their tender sensibilities. And the early
Pre-Raphaelites, though with somewhat greater self-con-
trol, likewise attempted to find appropriate modern themes;
most notably, Holman Hunt in "The Awakening Conscience" and Rossetti in its verse counterpart "Jenny" depicted the fallen woman as the pitiable victim of a loveless
materialism, the muse degraded by a crude modern environment. But their knowledge of the real industrial society was inadequate and uneasy, and their appetite for
richly elaborated detail drove them repeatedly, both in
paint and words, to seek subject and décor in other haunts
of the imagination. Later William Morris, who moved
from Pre-Raphaelite visions to a more immediate social and
economic awareness, resolutely rejected all art with modern
subject matter as a shameful compromise with modern ugliness; to record the present age was in some measure to
approve it; one should work only for the better world of
the future when a beautiful art might once again be possible. Such an attitude was not far removed from the frame
of mind in which Matthew Arnold described the present
function of criticism: "the true life of literature" depended

upon "a current of true and living ideas" as in the epochs
of Aeschylus and Shakespeare:

there is the promised land, towards which criticism can only
beckon. That promised land it will not be ours to enter, and we
shall die in the wilderness: but to have desired to enter it, to have
saluted it from afar, is already, perhaps, the best distinction among
contemporaries; it will certainly be the best title to esteem with
posterity.[12]

But in another mood Arnold felt that living for the promise
one would not see fulfilled meant a betrayal of life's present
process. "Puritanism," he said in *Culture and Anarchy*,
"was perhaps necessary to develop the moral fibre of the
English race, Nonconformity to break the yoke of ecclesi-
astical domination over men's minds and to prepare the way
for freedom of thought in the distant future; still, culture
points out that the harmonious perfection of generations of
Puritans and Nonconformists has been, in consequence,
sacrificed."[13] And years earlier he had had his Empedocles
ask whether man's present life of struggle, thought, and
love were after all really so small a thing

> That we must feign a bliss
> Of doubtful future date,
> And, while we dream on this,
> Lose all our present state,
> And relegate to worlds yet distant our repose?

The will to accept the challenge of man's present state
found its most vigorous early-Victorian sanction in the
heated prose of Thomas Carlyle. Though drawn at first to
literature and then, with more prophetic fire, to history,
Carlyle could not escape a sense of political responsibility
to his own time. While at work in the summer of 1842 on

the letters and speeches of Cromwell, he read disquieting reports of the immediate "condition of England" and heard a secret voice, he said, ever reminding him, "Thou, behold, thou too art of it—thou must be of it!"[14] He turned accordingly from the seventeenth century to the nineteenth, specifically to *Past and Present*, the most cogent of his social analyses, for, as he told Emerson, "My heart is sick and sore in behalf of my own poor generation."[15] His concern for the present, however, had been clear as early as "Signs of the Times,"[16] and the logic of his gospel had been developed with brilliance and intensity in *Sartor Resartus*. The latter traced its philosopher-hero's growth from the Everlasting No, the encompassing denial of purpose and value in an age of crass materialism, through the perspectives of the Centre of Indifference, to the Everlasting Yea, the final assent to the life of the spirit, a life to be fulfilled only in creative activity, in the whole-souled commitment to work: "Love not Pleasure; love God. This is the Everlasting Yea, wherein all contradiction is solved: wherein whoso walks and works, it is well with him. . . . Be no longer a Chaos, but a World, or even Worldkin. Produce! Produce! Were it but the pitifullest infinitesimal fraction of a Product, produce it, in God's name. . . . Work while it is called Today; for the Night cometh, wherein no man can work."

So by turns Biblical, Germanic, ironic, Carlyle preached his secular version of the apostle's admonition: "Behold, now is the accepted time; behold, now is the day of salvation." And many of his younger contemporaries heeded his call or at least shared something of his creed. In America Emerson, having secured the Boston publication of *Sartor* three years before its appearance in book form in England, proceeded to develop his own more democratic brand of transcendental activism, and Longfellow, whether or not he knew the book at the time, rhymed off a quite Carlylean message in his prosily earnest "Psalm of Life":

> Trust no Future, howe'er pleasant!
> Let the dead Past bury its dead!
> Act,—act in the living Present!
> Heart within, and God o'erhead!

In London Tennyson argued endlessly with Carlyle, yet allowed him to speak for himself as irascible old James in "The Golden Year," who insists that only fools and dreamers place the golden age in the past or future,

> "but well I know
> That unto him who works, and feels he works,
> This same grand year is ever at the doors."

Clough, a more convinced disciple, wrote didactic lyrics such as "Qui Laborat, Orat" pointing to dutiful work as the antidote to modern skepticism and despair. And Ruskin, to whom the mantle of the prophet descended long before Carlyle's old age, chose as the motto for his seal "TODAY, TODAY, TODAY"—with the familiar Scriptural caution in mind: "tacitly underlined to myself," he confessed, "with the warning, 'The night cometh when no man can work.'"[17]

Even the young Rossetti, though surely as much aesthete as moralist, was inclined to respect the Carlylean gospel as a proper response to the demand of the Victorian present. In an early trio of sonnets entitled "The Choice" he examined three possible approaches to the life of the day: the hedonistic, the ascetic, and the active—

> Eat thou and drink; to-morrow thou shalt die. . . .
> Watch thou and fear; to-morrow thou shalt die. . . .
> Think thou and act; to-morrow thou shalt die. . . .

Glossing the three poems, his brother William commented: "It is manifest . . . that Rossetti intends us to set aside the 'Eat thou and drink' theory of life, and not to accept without much reservation the 'Watch thou and pray' theory. 'Think thou and act' is what he abides by."[18] Certainly, we might agree, the third sonnet concludes its exemplary sentiment with a vivid image to describe an insatiable Faustian aspiration, a perspective that offers no stopping place for present thought:

> From this wave-washed mound
> Unto the furthest flood-brim look with me;
> Then reach on with thy thought till it be drown'd.
> Miles and miles distant though the last line be
> And though thy soul sail leagues and leagues beyond,
> Still, leagues beyond those leagues, there is more sea.

But the three may represent merely a young man's disinterested effort to sum up dramatically three possible attitudes, to explore at the outset of his career a possible range of choices. The second choice, in fact, could never for long have been Rossetti's, and it clearly had little appeal to the restless unascetic nineteenth century. But the first, despite his brother's assurance to the contrary, was never lightly set aside; however high may have been his regard for thought and action, he recognized the power of a sensuous hedonism, as the sestet of the first sonnet described it, in lines that anticipate his own most characteristic manner:

> Now kiss, and think that there are really those,
> My own high-bosomed beauty, who increase
> Care, gold, and care, and yet might choose our way!

> Through many days they toil; then comes a day
> They die not,—never having lived,—but cease;
> And round their narrow lips the mould falls close.[19]

And the hedonistic "way" of facing the present seemed to many Victorians, especially in the latter part of the period, a likely and even defensible alternative to the Carlylean.

Though almost completely ignored until Rossetti came upon a remaindered copy of the first edition,[20] *The Rubái-yát* had become by the eighteen nineties the most popular poem of the nineteenth century and the very breviary of epicurean hedonism. FitzGerald, who was at least as much responsible for its tone as Omar Khayyám, described the sweet sad monody as "a desperate sort of Thing, unfortunately found at the bottom of all thinking Men's minds; but made Music of." And indeed, beside most other reworkings of the ancient *carpe diem* motif, *The Rubáiyát* seems shaded by despair and anxiety, by a disenchantment more Victorian than Persian, a constant reminder of the dread and misgiving to be deliberately forgotten, the moral burden of "unborn Tomorrow and dead Yesterday" to be willfully set aside in a sensuous and ever-receding Today:

> Ah, take the Cash, and let the Credit go,
> Nor heed the rumble of a distant Drum! . . .

> Ah, my Beloved, fill the Cup that clears
> Today of past Regrets and future Fears. . . .

> Perplext no more with Human or Divine,
> Tomorrow's tangle to the winds resign. . . .

> Waste not your Hour, nor in the vain pursuit
> Of This and That endeavour and dispute. . . .

> The Moving Finger writes, and, having writ
> Moves on: nor all your Piety nor Wit
>   Shall lure it back to cancel half a Line,
> Nor all your Tears wash out a Word of it.

Ronsard urged his Hélène simply to reciprocate love before age withered life's roses; and Herrick joyously invited his virgins to gather rosebuds, to make much of time while youth and blood were warm. But *The Rubáiyát* concentrates less on the pleasures to be gained by snatching the moment than on the pains to be escaped, the regrets and fears, the perplexities and contentions of a disputatious age, the sense of responsibility guiltily remembered in the very act of evasion.

However remote and exotic the imagery, the mood of the poem must have seemed to the Victorians self-conscious, familiar, and modern. It was anticipated by Thackeray's Pendennis, and probably endorsed by Thackeray himself, as a rationalization of both acceptance and withdrawal: "I take the world as it is, and being of it, will not be ashamed of it. If the time is out of joint, have I any calling or strength to set it right?"[21] It recurred as part of Morris's "apology" for *The Earthly Paradise*, long before the day of Morris's commitment to social action:

> Dreamer of dreams, born out of my due time,
> Why should I strive to set the crooked straight?

And the frame of mind, the half-reluctant, half-defiant hedonism, persisted until the First World War had thoroughly shaken the last of sturdier Victorian values. We detect it in the desperate cheer of a wartime letter from D. H. Lawrence to Bertrand Russell: "One must learn to be happy and careless. . . . So let us have a good time to ourselves while the old world tumbles over itself. It is no good bothering. Nothing is born by taking thought."[22] Such an ethic of pleasure, so commingling disillusion and ill-concealed regret, scarcely existed at all before the self-torturing, time-obsessed nineteenth century.

But there was also among the Victorians a readier acceptance of life in the present, less anxious and apologetic, more assertive and even dutiful. At its most ebullient it animated Browning's plea for total engagement:

> How good is man's life, the mere living! how
> fit to employ
> All the heart and the soul and the senses
> forever in joy![23]

At its most cautious it moved Hopkins to recognize the necessity of living well the one temporal life man can live; as he confided to his watch,

> The telling time our task is; time's some part,
> Not all, but we were framed to fail and die—
> One spell and well that one.[24]

Unlike Browning, Hopkins at the outset, as in "The Habit of Perfection," declared his mistrust of pure sensuousness. Yet his most assured work bespeaks a high sensuous endowment that places him, with the other major Victorian poets, to a marked degree in the succession of Keats. And his great nature sonnets of the late seventies, especially "God's Grandeur," "The Starlight Night," "The Windhover," "Pied Beauty," "Hurrahing in Harvest," all given immediacy by the present tense,[25] elevate the intense sense impression to a sacramental act:

Summer ends now; now, barbarous in beauty, the
          stooks arise
    Around; up above, what wind-walks! what lovely
          behaviour
    Of silk-sack clouds! has wilder, wilful-wavier
    Meal-drift moulded ever and melted across skies?

I walk, I lift up, I lift up heart, eyes,
    Down all that glory in the heavens to glean our
          Saviour;
    And, éyes, héart, what looks, what lips yet
          gave you a
    Rapturous love's greeting of realer, of rounder
          replies?

On a much lower level, or at least with far less poetic consequence, the cult of intensity, the commitment to a fully
engaged perception of the here and now, led Arthur
Symons to a personal creed of sensation. "If ever there was
a religion of the eyes," he declared, "I have devoutly prac-
tised that religion. I noted every face that passed me on the
pavement; I looked into the omnibuses, the cabs, always
with the same eager hope of seeing some beautiful or interesting person, some gracious movement, a delicate expression, which would be gone if I did not catch it as it
went."[26] Symons, who began his career with a study of
Browning, may have sought to emulate Browning's ideal
poet, the walker of the Spanish city, observing all things,
tapping "the pavement with his cane, / Scenting the world,
looking it full in face." But his "very aesthetic" temper was
never much like Browning's euphoria; and his religion of
the eyes, in the nineties when he developed it, could find
intellectual sanction nearer home.

In their distinct though not unrelated attitudes toward
the intense moment, both Hopkins and Symons owed

something directly to the precept and example of Walter Pater—Hopkins as one who had been his student at Oxford, Symons as his avowed admirer and disciple. And Pater in fact, in his own fastidious, recessive manner, at a time when an aesthetic critic seemed more persuasive than a social prophet, exercised an authority over the late Victorians perhaps more restricted but hardly less compelling than that of Carlyle over an earlier generation.[27] Pater more consistently than any other—though often, as was his way, by obliquity and subtle innuendo—offered a philosophy of the personal present in the setting of the public present. Modern thought, he declared in the notorious "Conclusion" to *The Renaissance*, had come to regard "all things and principles of things as inconstant modes or fashions," and all sense of fixity and solidity as merely illusion created by language. Our physical life, he insisted, was a perpetual motion of processes and impulses, and our knowledge of the outside world consisted essentially of our wavering fitful impressions, which existed only in our passing awareness. To achieve the most intense impression possible accordingly became the great objective of living; to seize the moment, to transfix it, became an aesthetic duty—for "Every moment some form grows perfect in hand or face; some tone on the hills or the sea is choicer than the rest; some mood of passion or insight or intellectual excitement is irresistibly real and attractive to us,—for that moment only." To let the attention lapse, to miss even a single perfect form, was virtually to die a little, whereas "To burn always with this hard, gemlike flame, to maintain this ecstasy, [was] success in life." When Pater saw to his chagrin that these counsels of hedonism were being construed as a license for dangerous living ("Not the fruit of experience," he had written, "but experience itself, is the end"), he suppressed the "Conclusion" until he had refined the doctrine and explained it at length in *Marius the Epicurean*. The gospel now became the New Cyrenaicism, according to which one was to seek "not pleasure, but fullness of life, and 'insight' as conducting to that fullness—energy, variety, and choice of experience, including noble pain and sorrow even"; and the first commandment read: *"Be perfect in regard to what is here and now."*[28] Thus whatever the label, the philosophy set a high premium on the present impression, the life of immediate sensation.

Pater's guide to private conduct in the here and now gained cogency from his respect for the public present, his concern with the sensibility not just of the isolated artist but of the age itself. His *Renaissance* is less an art history than a study of the origins of the modern temper. The several essays that make up the volume keep returning to the subject of modernity: modern eclecticism, the modern cult of personality, the modern "consciousness brooding with delight over itself," the diversity of "the modern world, with its conflicting claims, its entangled interests, . . . so bewildering an experience, the problem of unity with ourselves"; and the essay on Michelangelo suggests that perhaps indeed "the chief use in studying old masters" is simply better to understand "the mixed, confused productions of the modern mind." The analysis of Leonardo is especially revealing: Leonardo is modern in that he makes time personal and subjective, "trifles with his genius, and crowds all his chief work into a few tormented years of later life"; his achievement as a whole, resting in large part on his own impressions and experiments, evinces "what is called the 'modern spirit,' with its realism, its appeal to experience"; and his Mona Lisa, in particular, expressive of the aggregate passions of mankind, stands as "the symbol of the modern idea," since it is modern philosophy that has "conceived the idea of humanity as wrought upon by, and summing up in itself, all modes of thought and life." Such descriptions frequently imply a judgment of value, an approval of the present time, or at least a sympathetic consideration of its character. Near the beginning of *Marius* Pater pictured his hero as exhilarated by the life of the city about him: "His entire rearing hitherto had lent itself to an imaginative exaltation of the past; but now the spectacle actually afforded to his untired and freely open senses, suggested the reflection that the present had, it might be, really advanced beyond the past, and he was ready to boast in the very fact that it was modern."[29] Pater himself seemed often to bask in the mere fact of modernity, to congratulate himself and his contemporaries on living in an age of innovation and open-minded or at least "open-sensed" response.

One of Marius's modernisms, we are told, was to keep a private diary, in which he might " 'confess himself,' with an intimacy, seemingly rare among the ancients." If only, Pater speculated, the great classical writers had given us an occasional hint of their own deepest selves, their inmost thoughts and feelings, we might often take double the interest in "their objective informations."[30] From such a proposition, Matthew Arnold would sharply have dissented; in objectivity, he believed, lay the abiding strength of the ancients, whereas increased introspection, "the dialogue of the mind with itself," had robbed the moderns of the power of delineating both object and action. The difference in their view of modern literature is indeed one of the main distinctions to be drawn between Arnold and Pater as critics. Yet Pater, for all his sympathy with modern modes and practices, saw the losses to life in the present as well as the gains. Modern man, he wrote, had a new and urgent need of the sense of freedom; the old assumptions of free will had been weakened, if not destroyed, by the deterministic forces of modern science, "the universality of natural law, even in the moral order." The great question now facing artist and critic was accordingly: "Can art represent men and women in these bewildering toils so as to give the spirit at least an equivalent for the sense of freedom?"[31] Arnold had reached a somewhat similar conclusion in his inaugural lecture as professor of poetry at Oxford: modern man required, he declared, "an intellectual deliverance," a mode of comprehending the "vast multitude of facts" exhibited by an age which "has around it a copious and complex present, and behind it a copious and complex past." Otherwise, as he told Clough some years earlier, one would be overwhelmed entirely by the present, "prevailed over by the world's multitudinousness."[32] Pater, unlike Arnold, was convinced that the best writers of the nineteenth century were already achieving the essential deliverance; but he nonetheless clearly understood the difficulty of their effort to attain the steadying "idea of the world" that Arnold demanded, and he sympathetically quoted the complaint of the retrospective Charles Lamb, "I cannot make these present times present to *me*."[33] The *carpe diem* philosophy might thus be severely attenuated if the day to be seized could not be imagined and defined with perfect clarity.

F. T. Palgrave of *The Golden Treasury*, much more conservative in his taste than Pater, was quite certain that "the vast complex organism of modern life" had distracted the graphic artist from any concern with infinite and eternal things and that "the glare of the present" was obscuring "those traditions and those aspirations in which fine art has always found its highest impulse."[34] And quite apart from painting altogether (even that like the work of the later Millais cynically produced simply to satisfy an immediate market[35]), a strong case can be made that, by the late Victorian period, the glare of the present was becoming intense enough effectively to obliterate any widespread serious concern with the public past or future. The new journalism of the nineties, at any rate, catering exclusively to the present, was making tradition seem irrelevant and foreshortening all possible prevision, with the consequence that many political and some cultural leaders, as all too often in the twentieth century, could plan only for short-term and short-sighted action.[36]

At the end of his life Marius came to feel that a true creed must resist all complacency with the present state of the material world and maintain "a kind of candid discontent, in the face of the very highest achievement."[37] Yet the Victorians, as their best literature never tires of telling us, were certainly subject to frequent moods of self-satisfaction—sometimes expressed with a naïveté rather appealing to a less assured posterity, as in the inscription on a memorial stone laid at the Tower Bridge in June 1886, "in the fiftieth year of HER MAJESTY's long, happy and prosperous reign." Dickens's Pip, who must have first come to London quite early in that reign, found even then a full measure of self-complacency: "We Britons had at that time particularly settled, that it was treasonable to doubt our having and our being the best of everything: otherwise, while I was scared by the immensity of London, I think I might have had some faint doubts whether it was not rather ugly, crooked, narrow and dirty."[38] And Arnold toward the middle of the reign was able to drench with his irony representative Victorian politicians, Sir Charles Adderley and Mr. Roebuck, who were extolling Englishmen as "the best breed in the whole world, . . . so superior to all the world," unrivaled in their happiness by any people "the world over or in past history."[39]

But not all the Victorians were always so blatantly wrong-headed in their regard for the contemporary. If many had a sense of their own difference as a generation, much of their present was in truth unprecedented. Their task was to apply or adapt the basic values of their civilization to an age of bewildering change. And whatever the late Victorian journalistic exploitation of the ephemeral, their major spokesmen, at least, retained until the end a respect for the historical past and a concern with the large concepts of progress and decadence. Their best commitment to the present, essential as it was to the direction of their own energies, was made with neither complacency nor despair, yet in the full consciousness of time.

~§ VIII §~

THE ETERNAL NOW

Or say that the end precedes the beginning,
And the end and the beginning were always there
Before the beginning and after the end.
And all is always now.
                                    –T. S. Eliot

As children by the sea at Yarmouth David Copperfield and little Em'ly naturally assume a world without
time and so make "no more provision for growing older,
than . . . for growing younger."[1] Miss Havisham of *Great
Expectations*, on the other hand, has made a vain, deliberate
effort to arrest time; she has stopped the clock in her room
at twenty minutes to nine; but the day has worn relentlessly on, the wedding gown has withered on her shrunken
body, and the bridal cake has long since mouldered.

Aware always of temporal relations and responsibilities,
no adult can contrive or decree the release from time that
the child habitually enjoys. Yet the desire for transcendence
remains, and the dream of eternity may often prove not
Miss Havisham's delusion but an enriching vision. In "The
Bridge Builders," as we have seen, Kipling pointed to the
necessity of a certain short-sightedness, if one were to keep
faith in the idea of material progress. In "The Brushwood
Boy," a more deeply personal story, he depicted a divided
modern sensibility. His hero George Cottar, a perfectly

137

efficient and apparently well-adjusted English official in India, does his dull duty with great charm and expedition, yet all the while leads a secret dream life far from the routine of his daily work and all the demands of "They" and "Them," the forces alien to his hidden self. Cottar is more fortunate than most dreamers, insofar as he eventually finds a sharer of his dream; on his return to England he meets a woman who for years has likewise imagined the timeless real life as beginning at a brushwood pile on a lonely beach. But many, lacking such fulfillment, have known only the weariness of time, as the pressures of the present closed in upon them.

In the last chapter of his *Biographia Literaria* Coleridge suggested that some intimation of eternity, gleaned from the perception of a causal nexus between events in human time, alone could make the temporal dimension and man's constant struggle in it seem meaningful. "The sense of Before and After," he wrote, "becomes both intelligible and intellectual when, and *only* when, we contemplate the succession in the relations of Cause and Effect, which, like the two poles of the magnet manifest the being and unity of the one power by relative opposites, and give, as it were, a substratum of permanence, of identity, and therefore of reality, to the shadowy flux of Time. It is Eternity revealing itself in the phenomena of Time: and the perception and acknowledgment of the proportionality and appropriateness of the Present to the Past, prove to the afflicted Soul, that it has not yet been deprived of the sight of God. . . ."[2]

All of the other major Romantic poets, though usually in less abstruse terms, were similarly concerned to discover tokens of permanence or stasis in or behind their passing impressions, and most came to regard their own deepest emotions and intuitions as partaking somehow of the timeless. And the Victorians who followed liked to trust with Shelley that the true poet participated in the infinite and the eternal. Arnold indeed insisted, in his preface of 1853, that poetry must treat of great actions, those "which most powerfully appeal to the great primary human affections: to those elementary feelings which subsist permanently in the race, and which are independent of time."[3] Yet he himself as poet was seldom able to achieve such independence. His preface was written to explain the suppression of *Empedocles on Etna*, which like most of his best work was "secondary" and sophisticated, timely and modern, in its sentiments. And Arnold's contemporaries generally were too conscious of the distinctions between past and present to believe that any very wide range of feelings was wholly beyond the touch of time. Coleridge's notion of an eternal substratum differs from most other nineteenth-century literary speculation on permanence in that it has the clearly religious context and significance we find repeatedly in earlier concern with eternity.

According to the traditional time-scheme of Christian orthodoxy, the Past was the period of the world's creation; the Present, the here and now of this mortal life; and the Future, the day of the Second Coming and apocalypse; Eternity entered human time at a precise juncture of history, the death and resurrection of Christ. Such a view seldom appears in Romantic or Victorian poetry, but it receives at least one striking expression, Hopkins's powerful lyric "That Nature is a Heraclitean Fire and of the Comfort of the Resurrection." The "Heraclitean Fire" suggests a possible derivation from Pater's "Conclusion" with its epigraph from Heraclitus and its pervasive fire imagery; and the first movement of the poem captures with incomparable vividness the Paterian sense of flame, flicker, and shifting light, the wonder of "nature's bonfire" constantly refueled, until the argument turns to consider the pathos of man's brief bright "spark," his little life in time:

> O pity and indignation! Manshape, that shone
> Sheer off, disseveral, a star, / death blots black out; nor mark
>   Is any of him at all so stark
> But vastness blurs and time / beats level.

Then suddenly remembrance of the Resurrection—a comfort Pater does not consider—"an eternal beam," destroys time, blots out with greater light the "world's wildfire," and

>   In a flash, at a trumpet crash,
> I am all at once what Christ is, / since he was what I am, and
> This Jack, joke, poor potsherd, / patch, matchwood, immortal diamond
>   Is immortal diamond.

In poets less responsive to the appeal of dogmatic theology, the concept of a religious eternity was necessarily less precise. Tennyson's mystical or quasi-mystical experience defied translation into concrete terms; as in his early "Armageddon," so in all his moments of tranced vision,

>   All sense of Time
> And Being and Place was swallowed up
> Within a victory of boundless thought.

Browning, despite his devotion to the process of living in the world of sharp sense impressions, could apparently endorse the somewhat bullying abstractions of his Rabbi Ben Ezra,

> Fool! All that is, at all,
> Lasts ever, past recall . . .

or of his Renaissance grammarian,

> What's time? Leave Now for dogs and apes!
> Man has Forever.[4]

And Swinburne could assign an elusive everlastingness, beyond "time-stricken lands," to his vague earth-goddess Hertha. But with the general questioning and inevitable weakening of religious sanctions throughout the nineteenth century, faith in an eternal order became for many more and more precarious, and the idea of eternity, often almost completely secularized, grew correspondingly personal and psychological.

Rossetti, who strove to find a substitute religion in physical love, trusted that the intense sense experience might perhaps grant the lover the nearest possible approach to a conquest of time:

> And shall my sense pierce love,—the last relay
> And ultimate outpost of eternity?[5]

And Arnold, though more tentatively, suggested that in rare moments of reciprocated sympathy between man and woman—"When a beloved hand is laid in ours,"—a man might achieve peace of spirit and even some sense of an eternal dimension:

> And there arrives a lull in the hot race
> Wherein he doth forever chase
> That flying and elusive shadow, rest.
> An air of coolness plays upon his face,
> And an unwonted calm pervades his breast.
> And then he thinks he knows
> The hills where his life rose,
> And the sea where it goes.[6]

But in neither poet is there complete certitude; Rossetti asks hopefully whether the sense can actually reach the timeless essence of love, and Arnold allows the lover not precisely to know, but to *think* he knows, the eternity imaged by sea and hills.

Others looked to nature itself, rather than to human passion, for warranty of a permanence beyond time. Wordsworth—to cite the most memorable example—had seen the apparently static subsuming the strongly dynamic in the mountain majesty of the Simplon Pass, where the woods decaying would never be decayed and the blasts of waterfalls were so constant as to seem stationary; and he found in the total harmony "Characters of the great Apocalypse, / The types and symbols of Eternity, / Of first, and last, and midst, and without end."[7] And the young Ruskin shared Wordsworth's response to mountain scenery: "What more, what else," he wondered, "could be asked of seemingly immutable good in this mutable world?"[8] But Wordsworth, especially after his brother John's death by drowning in a storm at sea, learned to suspect nature's benevolence; and Ruskin, haunted by time and change, grew convinced that the "seemingly immutable" was simply fond illusion. As the nineteenth century continued, nature became less and less available as an object of veneration.[9] The Darwinian view of the natural world corroborated Tennyson's description of nature as "red in tooth and claw," and the new scientists, whether biological or geological, would have accepted his picture of the solid hills as flowing from form to form and indeed of all nature as committed to destructive change:

> "So careful of the type?" but no,
>   From scarpèd cliff and quarried stone
>   She cries, "A thousand types are gone;
> I care for nothing, all shall go."[10]

By the end of the Victorian period, the floral style in the graphic arts, known as the *art nouveau*, might perhaps be construed as a highly contrived effort to relate the design of a rapidly moving industrial society to elemental and enduring natural forms. But in literature the motifs from nature that still remained seldom carried connotations of eternity.

"What is eternal? What escapes decay?": the aesthetic Arthur O'Shaughnessy answered the question with a brave will to believe—if all else failed—in art, in "a certain faultless, matchless, deathless line / Curving consummate."[11] Whistler agreed: on a Japanese fan he found all perfect and timeless; the true artist, devoted only to tone and arrangement, had no conceivable interest in the progress or decadence of his society.[12] Professing a similar creed, the late Victorian literary aesthetes turned for sanction not to Hokusai but to the theory and practice of the French Parnassians, especially Théophile Gautier, whose "L'Art" Austin Dobson admirably translated:

> All passes. Art alone
>   Enduring stays to us;
> The Bust outlasts the throne,—
>   The Coin, Tiberius;
>
> Even the gods must go;
>   Only the lofty Rhyme
> Not countless years o'erthrow,—
>   Not long array of time.

Taking a more realistic view, the aged Tennyson in "Parnassus" denied the perdurability of any rhyme, shaped as all verse must be under the ironic gaze of the "terrible Muses," Astronomy and Geology. Yet even Tennyson would grant that art had greater longevity than most other things short-lived and human; and even if the art work itself were not eternal, it might suggest, as long as it did endure, timeless values and archetypes, images of stasis like his own Sleeping Beauty, "A perfect form in perfect rest." Arnold imagined his scholar-gypsy as immortal because a literary artifact, "exempt from age / And living as thou liv'st on Glanvil's page," and he pictured a hunter on a tapestry in "Tristram and Iseult," forever alert, forever rooted in the greenwood, gazing out at the dead lovers in a bleak chamber. All such considerations of the power of art to arrest the moment (and they have been frequent in Victorian and modern literature, where one of the main themes of poetry is the nature of poetry itself) recall Keats's superb evocation of the youth and beauty frozen forever on the Grecian urn, the wild ecstasy that will not tire, the leaves that cannot fall. But none repeats the miracle of the ode, which in its ultimate proportion remains, like the urn itself, a silent form able to "tease us out of thought, / As doth eternity."

Though concerned—at least until late in the period—more with the content than the design of art, the Victorians from the beginning were highly self-conscious stylists, deliberately eclectic in their selection of motifs or turns of phrase. Hopkins commended Swinburne for making an effort "at establishing a new standard of poetic diction," but complained that the new language was "essentially archaic" and so ineffective— "now that is a thing that can never last: a perfect style must be of its age."[13] Yet Hopkins himself shaped a new diction at least as rich in archaisms and root meanings as in contemporary idiom. Stylistic eclecticism, though born of a greatly widened response to history, was no doubt intended throughout the nineteenth century to suggest that art was independent of the age and virtually above time altogether. The art work was to be presented "in weird devices," like the enchanted gate of Camelot, with

> New things and old co-twisted, as if Time
> Were nothing, so inveterately that men
> Were giddy gazing there.[14]

But whether or not it could evoke a sense of eternity by style alone, art could clearly seek out a timeless subject matter. Occasionally the poets strove to construct worlds of artifice beyond the reach of change. Morris's *Earthly Paradise*, the longest of such efforts, expressly undertook "to build a shadowy isle of bliss / Midmost the beating of the steely sea." Swinburne's "Forsaken Garden" fancifully depicted a ghostly tract where, all life vegetable and human having already died, death could "deal not again forever," nor change come "till all change end." And Tennyson's "Recollections of the Arabian Nights" conjured up a realm "Apart from place, withholding time," while his "Lotos-Eaters" reproduced the breathless quiet of an unending afternoon in "A land where all things always seemed the same." But Tennyson was too deeply engrossed by the meaning of his own past and the needs of a public present to escape for long into the timeless illusion he could so readily create. And the dominant literary mode of the century—especially in prose fiction, though not without its effect on poetry, too—was a "realism" rooted in the particulars of place and time.

Ruskin, who sought "truth to nature" above all else, asked that the artist, working preferably with his eye on the object, "stay what is fleeting . . . and immortalize the things that have no duration."[15] In other words, intimations of eternity were to be found in the matter of direct experience. Pater developed a similar notion in his essay on

Giorgione. "Now it is part of the ideality of the highest
sort of dramatic poetry," he wrote, "that it presents us
with a kind of profoundly significant and animated in-
stants, a mere gesture, a look, a smile, perhaps—some brief
and wholly concrete moment—into which, however, all
the motives, all the interests and effects of a long history,
have condensed themselves, and which seem to absorb past
and future in an intense consciousness of the present."[16]
Pater called these heightened moments "exquisite pauses in
time"; Wordsworth, more simply, spoke of "spots of time";
Joyce, more recondrtely, of "epiphanies"; all three described what has become a major concern in modern literature.

   Stephen Hero defines an epiphany as "a sudden spiritual
manifestation, whether in the vulgarity of speech or in a
memorable phrase of the mind itself"; and *A Portrait of the
Artist* makes it clear that the revelation brings a sense of
timeless harmony, "the luminous silent stasis of esthetic
pleasure, a spiritual state very like to that cardiac condition
which the Italian physiologist Luigi Galvani . . . called the
enchantment of the heart."[17] *The Prelude*, as we should
expect, links the spot of time to Wordsworth's psychology
of memory; the experience reanimates life with purpose,
and its remembrance proves an abiding restorative:

> There are in our existence spots of time,
> That with distinct pre-eminence retain
> A renovating virtue, whence—depressed
> By false opinion and contentious thought,
> Or aught of heavier or more deadly weight,
> In trivial occupations, and the round
> Of ordinary intercourse—our minds
> Are nourished and invisibly repaired.

As an example, Wordsworth recounts an incident recollected from early boyhood, his being separated from his guide in a lonely valley, his flight in terror from an abandoned gibbet, and then his "reascending the bare common" and seeing

> A naked pool that lay beneath the hills,
> The beacon on the summit, and, more near,
> A girl, who bore a pitcher on her head,
> And seemed with difficult steps to force her way
> Against the blowing wind.

This, he assures us, was quite an "ordinary sight"; yet the whole scene fell suddenly into so sharpened a focus that it was invested forever with a "visionary dreariness" beyond description. Perceiving a unity greater by far than the sum of the separate impressions, the mind thus asserted its rightful place as "lord and master" over "outward sense." In an earlier passage, introducing the description of the Simplon Pass and the sense of eternity its magnificence engendered, the faculty of mind that effects such transformations is explicitly identified as the imagination, and the moment of insight is given the most decisive spiritual significance:

> in such strength
> Of usurpation, when the light of sense
> Goes out, but with a flash that has revealed
> The invisible world, doth greatness make abode,
> There harbors; whether we be young or old,
> Our destiny, our being's heart and home,
> Is with infinitude, and only there;
> With hope it is, hope that can never die,
> Effort, and expectation, and desire,
> And something evermore about to be.[18]

Though based on sense perception until the light of sense yields a brighter illumination, the spot of time thus accords with Wordsworth's essentially religious impulse; it seems to fulfill the desire for everlastingness, for a continuity beyond both sense and time. In the moment of revelation the physical outline, preternaturally sharpened, wavers, and the object suddenly, like the aged Leech-gatherer, partakes of eternity:

> the whole body of the man did seem
> Like one whom I had met with in a dream;
> Or like a man from some far region sent,
> To give me human strength, by apt admonishment. . . .
>
> In my mind's eye I seemed to see him pace
> About the moors continually,
> Wandering about alone and silently.

Despite its derivation as a term from the Christian calendar, the Joycean epiphany scarcely goes so far in religious implication. Yet it represents a modern artist's will to find in the aesthetic perception of life something of an assurance of value otherwise denied to a secular age; it offers, at least for the moment, the "silent stasis," the possibility of a fixed and ultimate pattern. Such was the meaning of the spot of time, with varying degrees of metaphysical association, to many writers between Wordsworth and Joyce. Rossetti, for example, conceived of the sonnet as "a moment's monument, / Memorial from the Soul's eternity / To one dead deathless hour," and celebrated in the form blest moments like the silent noon of shared understanding, "this winged hour . . . dropped to us from above":

Oh! clasp we to our hearts, for deathless dower,
This close-companioned inarticulate hour
When twofold silence was the song of love.[19]

Meredith presented the moment of insight as a cherished substitute for a lost eternity; the husband in *Modern Love* remembers an hour of brief reconciliation when he and his estranged wife, both for once released from thoughts of their own past and future, caught an image of selfless, timeless harmony:

Love, that had robbed us of immortal things,
This little moment mercifully gave
Where I have seen across the twilight wave
The swan sail with her young beneath her wings.

And Browning, always more intrigued by movement than by stasis, apparently found spots of time in moments of high aspiration when the goal was in sight but still unattained; the lover, at any rate, in "The Last Ride Together" is able to imagine heaven itself as merely a continuation of the ride, a perpetual extension of his life's unfulfilled mission:

And yet—she has not spoke so long!
What if heaven be that, fair and strong
At life's best, with our eyes upturned
Whither life's flower is first discerned,
    We, fixed so, ever should so abide?
What if we still ride on, we two,
With life forever old yet new,
Changed not in kind but in degree,
The instant made eternity—
And heaven just prove that I and she
    Ride, ride together, forever ride?

In *Marius the Epicurean* Pater offers several instances of what he must have meant by the exquisite pause in time. Once, when delayed at an inn, Marius rests in an olive-garden, where he sees far below him, and as if in a dream, the road he has been traveling and perceives suddenly in "this peculiar and privileged hour" the true direction of his whole life and the possibility of a real world beyond time "in which the experiences he valued most might find, one by one, an abiding place." But the most vivid illumination vouchsafed to Marius cannot be so readily translated into abstract metaphysical or moral terms. It is simply an impression that accompanies the sight of his friend Cornelius gleaming in golden armor, in an "odd interchange of light and shade": Marius, sensitive to every detail in the aesthetic arrangement, feels instantly and apocalyptically "as if he were face to face, for the first time, with some new knighthood or chivalry, just then coming into the world."[20] The pause in the garden brings the sort of revelation that should rightly precede a conversion (like that of Teufelsdröckh in *Sartor Resartus*), though Marius remains always too ambivalent to make the final commitment of faith. The vision of Cornelius, on the other hand, is little more than the brief moment that gives added dimension to everyday experience; it is the kind of epiphany we encounter frequently in Victorian and later prose fiction. Mordecai in *Daniel Deronda*—to cite a rather close parallel —beholds Deronda rowing down the Thames toward him, river and rower alike transfigured by the evening light, and feels "in that moment . . . his inner prophecy . . . fulfilled"; Deronda is clearly the ideal young leader he has been looking for, and "Obstacles, incongruities, all melted into the sense of completion with which his soul was flooded by this outward satisfaction of his longing."[21] Similarly Marlow in *Lord Jim,* as he sends Jim off to Patusan, shares with the young man "a moment of real and profound intimacy, unexpected and short-lived, like a glimpse of some everlasting, of some saving truth."[22] To Virginia Woolf, every such moment was a visitation of reality, a sudden unequivocal insight into the heart of life. As everywhere in her own novels, "reality," so understood, is that which "lights up a group in a room or stamps some casual saying, . . . overwhelms one walking home beneath the stars and makes the silent world more real than the world of speech"; indeed, "whatever it touches, it fixes and makes permanent."[23]

Before the nineteenth century, reality was seldom to be defined in such terms. Men long before Wordsworth had, of course, experienced sudden and sometimes soul-shattering revelation. But the spot of time, the private and personal epiphany, took on a new meaning in an age with new concepts of public time, an age with a new awareness of history and obsessive notions of cultural progress and decadence. Troubled by constant change throughout society, by precipitant onward movement often without apparent pattern or direction, the post-Romantic artist might concentrate attention on the qualitative time of the individual and, in doing so, seek to withdraw altogether from the bewildering drift of public affairs. Rossetti is a striking case in point. In his concern with the "moment's monument" that was art, Rossetti grew more and more convinced of "the momentary momentousness and eternal futility of many noisiest questions."[24] John Morley, who was above all the political man, told of meeting him once at the crisis of a general election, and of his declaring a total ignorance of the campaign and remarking that "no doubt one side or the other would get in" and it would make little or no difference which.[25] Later his young protégé Hall Caine was somewhat shocked by his confession: "To speak without sparing myself,—my mind is a childish one, if to be isolated in Art is child's play."[26] Yet not even Rossetti could escape time. Far from being wholly isolated, he was painfully aware of the judgments of his contemporaries; and he suffered—to the point of nervous collapse—the feeling of "being hounded out of society" by Robert Buchanan's *Fleshly School*, an attack which an independent artist should simply have laughed off or ignored.[27] For all his escapist gestures, he was always in large part the product and the victim of the public time he strove to forget.

Rossetti's retreat dramatizes a common and often necessary reaction to a world that was indeed too much with all nineteenth-century men, the world of getting and spending, late and soon, where time was money, the measure of material gain. Yet if the artist could not in fact wholly transcend the age, he could still detach himself long enough and far enough to attempt to see life in some perspective, steadily and whole, beyond what was merely current and timely. And his work could remind men of the quality of the individual life, as well as of its obvious brevity. Cities and Thrones and Powers, as Kipling put it, endured "in Time's eye" scarcely longer than the flower; yet all could learn a salutary truth from the latter, which lived beautifully in the assumption of perpetuity:

> This season's Daffodil,
>   She never hears
> What change, what chance, what chill,
>   Cut down last year's;
>
> But with bold countenance,
>   And knowledge small,
> Esteems her seven days' continuance
>   To be perpetual.[28]

Finally, by examining the intense and privileged moment, art, especially poetry, might suggest that time itself, as man reckons it, was after all man's own invention, a device for dividing eternity into negotiable parts; for

> we, thin minds, who creep from thought to thought
> Break into "Thens" and "Whens" the Eternal Now—
> This double seeming of the single world![29]

If it could restore even briefly a sense of integration, unity, and design, art could reduce to harmless illusion the terror of time, the separation of then and when, before and after. Modern man might then return to the facts of change and history, progress and decadence, private past and public present, with an unproven yet sustaining conviction of continuity. The triumph of time, apparently assured and imperious, was actually never complete as long as anyone could question the first premises of its being.

NOTES

NOTES

The passages from "Burnt Norton" by T. S. Eliot used as epigraphs to Chapters VI and VIII have been quoted from T. S. Eliot's *Four Quartets* by permission of Faber and Faber, Ltd., London, and Harcourt, Brace and World, Inc., New York. All quotations from Gerard Manley Hopkins and the lines from Dobson's translation of Gautier are drawn by permission of the Oxford University Press from the *Poems of Gerard Manley Hopkins* and the *Complete Poetical Works of Austin Dobson*. Quotations from Hardy's verse, *The Collected Poems of Thomas Hardy*, are included by permission of Macmillan and Company, Ltd., London, The Macmillan Company of Canada, and The Macmillan Company, New York. Two quatrains from Housman's *Shropshire Lad* appear with permission granted by The Society of Authors as the literary representatives of the Estate of the late A. E. Housman, and Messrs. Jonathan Cape, Ltd., publishers of A. E. Housman's *Collected Poems*. The lines from "Cities and Thrones and Powers" in Chapter VIII are reproduced from Kipling's *Puck of Pook's Hill* by permission of Mrs. George Bambridge, the poet's daughter, and Macmillan and Company, Ltd., London, and by arrangement with Doubleday and Company, Inc., New York, publishers of *Rudyard Kipling's Verse: Definitive Edition*.

When two dates are given in parentheses following a title, the first indicates date of first publication, the second the date of the edition I have used. Passages from novels are identified simply by chapter number. Well-known poems are cited merely by title or, if the title occurs in the text itself introducing the quotation, not included in the notes at all.

PREFACE

1. John Stuart Mill, *The Spirit of the Age* (1831: Chicago, University of Chicago Press, 1942), p. 1.
2. G. Kitson Clark, *The Making of Victorian England* (Cambridge, Harvard University Press, 1962), p. 58.

CHAPTER I. THE FOUR FACES OF VICTORIAN TIME

1. "The Mystic" appeared in Tennyson's first independent book, *Poems, Chiefly Lyrical* (1830) and was thereafter suppressed. But an even earlier piece, "Time: An Ode," had been included among Alfred's contributions to *Poems by Two Brothers* (1827).

2. Arnold, "Literature and Science" (1882), *Discourses in America* (London, 1885), p. 135.

3. Swinburne, "The Lake of Gaube" (1899).

4. Ruskin, *Time and Tide, Works,* Library Edition, 39 vols. (London, Allen, 1903-1912), XVII, 395-396.

5. Carlyle, *Sartor Resartus, Works,* Centenary Edition, 30 vols. (London, 1896), I, 103-104; cf. *Heroes and Hero-Worship, Works,* V, 8.

6. Wyndham Lewis, *Time and Western Man* (Boston, Beacon Press, 1957), p. 433; cited also in Geoffrey Wagner's *Wyndham Lewis: A Portrait of the Artist as the Enemy* (London, Routledge, 1957), p. 163.

7. Cf. Hans Meyerhoff's observation that in the nineteenth century "all the sciences of man—biology, anthropology, psychology, even economics and politics—became 'historical' sciences in the sense that they recognized and employed a historical, genetic, or evolutionary method." *Time in Literature* (Berkeley, University of California Press, 1955), p. 97.

8. Hardy, " 'So, Time,' " a continuation of "The Absolute Explains" (which argues that science has made a mockery of Time), dated 1922, *Collected Poems* (New York, Macmillan, 1928), p. 723. On the modern scientific view of time, see Hans Reichenbach, *The Direction of Time* (Berkeley, University of California Press, 1956).

9. William Whewell, *History of Scientific Ideas,* 2 vols. (London, 1858), I, 133.

10. Thackeray, *Esmond,* Book II, Chapter I.

11. Stevenson, "The Lantern-Bearers," *Works,* 25 vols. (London, Chatto and Windus, 1912), XVI, 207.

12. Pater, "Conclusion," *The Renaissance* (1873: New York, Modern Library, n.d.), pp. 195-196.

13. Harrison, "A Few Words about the Nineteenth Century," *The Choice of Books* (London, Macmillan, 1907), p. 424; the essay first appeared in *Fortnightly Review,* April 1882.

14. Carlyle, "Shooting Niagara," *Works,* XXX, 2-3.

15. See *The Education of Henry Adams* (Boston, Houghton

Mifflin, 1918), p. 380, and for Adams' "rule of phase," see his *Degradation of the Democratic Dogma* (1919: New York, Smith, 1949).

16. *Sartor Resartus, Works,* I, 188. I have discussed the concern of Carlyle and others with spiritual rebirth in "The Pattern of Conversion," *The Victorian Temper* (Cambridge, Harvard University Press, 1951), pp. 87–108.

17. Ruskin, "The Nature of Gothic," *The Stones of Venice, Works,* X, 214.

18. Clough, "Ah! Yet Consider It Again" (1851), the first stanza of which runs:

"Old things need not be therefore true."
O brother men, nor yet the new;
Ah! still awhile the old thought retain,
And yet consider it again!

19. Tennyson, "Love Thou Thy Land" (1834) and "To the Queen" (1872), epilogue to *Idylls of the King.*

20. Arnold, quotations from "The Function of Criticism at the Present Time" (1864), "The Scholar-Gypsy" (1853), "Stanzas in Memory of the Author of 'Obermann'" (1849), "Resignation" (1849).

21. Arthur O'Shaughnessy, "Ode" (1874), where poets are pictured as above time in all ages, prophesying things to come, "the dreamers of dreams," yet "the movers and shakers / Of the world forever."

CHAPTER II. THE USES OF HISTORY

1. Morris, *News from Nowhere* (1890: London, Longmans, 1935), p. 34.

2. Morris, "How I Became a Socialist" (1894), *Works,* 24 vols. (London, Longmans, 1915), XXIII, 280.

3. See esp. Nikolaus Pevsner, *Pioneers of Modern Design: From William Morris to Walter Gropius* (London, Penguin Books, 1960).

4. Morley, *On Compromise* (1874: London, Macmillan, 1928), p. 95.

5. Ruskin, *The Seven Lamps of Architecture, Works,* VIII, 234.

6. Ruskin, "Traffic," *The Crown of Wild Olive, Works,* XVIII, 455.

7. Morris, "Some Hints on Pattern Designing," *Works*, XXII, 180.

8. See F. J. Levy, "The Founding of the Camden Society," *Victorian Studies*, VII (1964), 295–305.

9. On Arnold's various sources, see C. B. Tinker and H. F. Lowry, *The Poetry of Matthew Arnold* (London, Oxford University Press, 1940).

10. Macaulay, "History," *Critical, Historical and Miscellaneous Essays and Poems*, 3 vols. (Boston, n.d.), I[1], 412. Cf. Lewis Mumford's comment, "From the Jews, the Greeks needed to learn about the meaningfulness of time, change, and history," *The Transformations of Man* (New York, Harper, 1956), p. 230.

11. Henley, "Essays and Essayists," *Works*, 7 vols. (London, Nutt, 1908), V, 229.

12. Morley, *On Compromise*, pp. 18–20.

13. See Gordon Haight, ed., *The George Eliot Letters*, 7 vols. (New Haven, Yale University Press, 1954, 1955), I, 206, letter from Mrs. Charles Bray to Sara Hennell: "She said she was Strauss-sick—it made her ill dissecting the beautiful story of the crucifixion, and only the sight of her Christ-image and picture made her endure it." Cf. I, 185, 197.

14. Browning, "Christmas-Eve," sec. XV, *Christmas-Eve and Easter Day* (1850).

15. Seeley, *Ecce Homo* (1865: Boston, 1896), p. 3

16. Hopkins, "The Wreck of the Deutschland," lines 47, 49–50, *Poems* (New York, Oxford University Press, 1948), p. 57.

17. Pattison, "Tendencies of Religious Thought in England, 1688–1750," *Essays and Reviews* (1860: Boston, 1862), p. 280.

18. Newman, *An Essay on the Development of Christian Doctrine* (1845: New York, Longmans, 1949), p. 7.

19. Josef L. Altholz, "Newman and History," *Victorian Studies*, VII (1964), 287.

20. Acton, quoted by Altholz, p. 288, from a manuscript in Cambridge University Library.

21. Newman, *The Idea of a University* (1852: New York, Longmans, 1947), p. 84; also cited by Altholz, p. 289.

22. Newman, "Mr Kingsley's Method of Disputation," Appendix II, *Apologia pro Vita Sua* (New York, Longmans, 1947), p. 374.

23. Mill, quoted by Michael St. John Packe, *The Life of John Stuart Mill* (New York, Macmillan, 1954), p. 268. As a dedicated reformer, Mill did of course believe that human progress was pos-

sible and that political institutions could and should be changed to meet new conditions, but he nonetheless had no notion that social change was effected by adaptation, or the process of "organic" growth—to use the biological metaphor invoked by later Victorian sociologists.

24. See Margaret Cole, *Beatrice Webb* (New York, Harcourt Brace, 1946), p. 36.

25. Macaulay, "Lord Bacon" (1837), *Essays*, II¹, 477, 478, 479, 488.

26. Huxley, "The Method by Which the Causes of the Present and Past Conditions of Organic Nature Are to Be Discovered," *Darwiniana, Selected Works* (New York, Appleton, n.d.), p. 361.

27. Lyell, *Principles of Geology*, 3 vols. (London, 1833), III, 384.

28. *In Memoriam*, sec. XXXV.

29. Ruskin, letter of May 24, 1851, to Henry Acland, *Works*, XXVI, 115.

30. See Glyn Daniel, *A Hundred Years of Archaeology* (London, Duckworth, 1950), and *The Idea of Prehistory* (London, Penguin Books, 1964).

31. Evans, quoted by Daniel, *Idea of Prehistory*, p. 45.

32. See Hans Meyerhoff's comments on "historicism" introducing his anthology, *The Philosophy of History in Our Time* (Garden City, Doubleday, 1959), p. 13.

33. J. A. Froude, "The Science of History," *Short Studies on Great Subjects* (New York, 1868), pp. 12, 34. Cf. Macaulay's hope that history would become like fiction: "a truly great historian would reclaim those materials which the novelist has appropriated" (*Essays*, I¹, 429).

34. Cf. Meyerhoff, *Philosophy of History*, p. 11.

35. Cf. E. H. Carr, *What is History?* (London, Penguin Books, 1964), p. 43: "History was full of meaning for British historians, so long as it seemed to be going our way; now that it has taken a wrong turning, belief in history has become a heresy."

36. Reade, *The Martyrdom of Man*, tenth edition (London, 1885), p. 543.

37. R. G. Collingwood, *The Idea of History* (New York, Oxford University Press, 1956), pp. 164–165; cf. also p. 327: "This distinction between periods of primitiveness, periods of greatness, and periods of decadence, is not and never can be historically true. It tells us much about the historians who study the facts, but nothing about the facts they study."

38. Ruskin, a *Fors Clavigera* letter of 1877, *Works*, XXIX, 224.

CHAPTER III. THE IDEA OF PROGRESS

1. Macaulay, "Sir James Mackintosh," *Essays*, II[1], 272, 279–280.
2. "Southey's Colloquies on Society," *Essays*, I[2], 183–184.
3. "Lord Bacon," *Essays*, II[1], 462–463.
4. Address delivered March 21, 1850, when plans were being laid for the Great Exhibition, *The Principal Speeches and Addresses of H. R. H. the Prince Consort* (London, 1862), p. 110.
5. Among the meanings of "future," the *Oxford English Dictionary* lists "a condition in time to come different (esp. in a favourable sense) from the present" and offers an 1852 citation as the earliest example of this usage.
6. Morris, "How I Became a Socialist," *Works*, XXIII, 279.
7. See R. J. Forbes and E. J. Dijksterhuis, *A History of Science and Technology*, 2 vols. (London, Penguin Books, 1963), the second volume of which covers, roughly, the period from 1750 to 1900; and, in much more detail, what is now the standard work on the subject, Charles Singer *et al.*, eds., *A History of Technology*, 5 vols. (New York, Oxford University Press, 1954–1958), the fourth volume covering the period from 1750 to 1850, and the fifth (888 pp.) devoted to the last half of the nineteenth century. The rate of acceleration has been such that the editors of the latter history do not venture to touch twentieth-century technology.
8. This is the complaint of Sigfried Giedion, *Space, Time and Architecture* (Cambridge, Harvard University Press, 1962), pp. 9–10.
9. See David Thomson, *England in the Nineteenth Century* (London, Penguin Books, 1950), and G. Kitson Clark, *The Making of Victorian England*, pp. 28–64. Clark comments that many of the Victorians were "just emerging from the animalism and brutality of primitive instincts" (p. 64).
10. Preface to a cheap edition of *Pickwick*, undated in later reprints, but originally dated (as Professor Edgar Johnson informs me) "September, 1847."
11. Lucretius, exceptionally, does suggest a progress in the arts, though he has no notion of a force leading inevitably to future improvement. On the idea of progress and its origins, much has been written, but see esp. F. S. Marvin, ed., *Progress and History* (Oxford, Humphrey Milford, 1917), J. B. Bury, *The Idea of Progress* (London, Macmillan, 1920), and Wilson D. Wallis, *Culture and Progress* (New York, Whittlesey House, 1930).

12. Turgot, quoted by Marvin, p. 15. On the French apologists for progress, see also Frank E. Manuel, *The Prophets of Paris* (Cambridge, Harvard University Press, 1962).

13. Guizot, quoted by Bury, *The Idea of Progress*, p. 274.

14. Gibbon, *History of the Decline and Fall of the Roman Empire*, J. B. Bury, ed., 7 vols. (New York, Macmillan, 1914), IV, 181. In his stimulating essay *What is History?* E. H. Carr explains why it would be ill-advised to regard this familiar passage as in any way ironical, since Gibbon clearly subscribed to the idea of progress common to the late eighteenth century.

15. See Gertrude Himmelfarb, *Lord Acton* (Chicago, University of Chicago Press, 1952), pp. 71, 196–197. Providential views of history, of course, persisted throughout the century among the orthodox; see, for example, the Anglican hymn (1894) by Canon A. C. Ainger:

> God is working his purpose out
> As year succeeds to year:
> God is working his purpose out,
> And the time is drawing near;
> Nearer and nearer draws the time,
> The time that shall surely be,
> When the earth shall be filled with the glory of God
> As the waters cover the sea.

16. Walter Bagehot, *Physics and Politics* (New York, Knopf, 1948), p. 226.

17. Harrison, *The Choice of Books*, pp. 421, 425.

18. Cf. the judgment of Christopher Dawson, writing in 1924, when the idea of progress seemed to him forever discredited: "From the second quarter of the eighteenth century onwards through the nineteenth, faith in human progress became more and more the effective working 'religion' of our civilization"—Dawson, *The Dynamics of World History* (New York, Sheed-Ward, 1957), p. 34. Cf. also R. G. Collingwood, *The Idea of History*, p. 144. Among the most sanguine books on the "law of progress" is *The Ethics of Progress* (London, Williams-Norgate, 1909) by Charles F. Dole, who writes: "There is an everlasting push of the universe bringing evil practices to nought, and slowly but surely, making the better things to prevail" (p. 393). See also Thomas S. Blair, *Human Progress—What Man Can Do to Further It* (New York, 1896).

19. Bury, *The Idea of Progress*, pp. vii, 5. Bury was not alone in his optimism even in the twenties; cf. J. O. Hertzler, *The History of Utopian Thought* (New York, Macmillan, 1923), p. 313: "We now have been able to develop a technique of social change, which we trust will in time make it possible more and more to correct man's faults, and remedy his weaknesses."

20. See Bury, p. 73.

21. Clifford, in a symposium on the decline of theology, *Nineteenth Century*, I (1877), 358.

22. Frederick Temple, "The Education of the World," *Essays and Reviews*, p. 3.

23. *In Memoriam*, sec. CXIV.

24. Thomas Chalmers, "The Christian Revelation Viewed in Connexion with the Modern Astronomy" (1817), Howard Mumford Jones and I. Bernard Cohen, eds., *A Treasury of Scientific Prose* (Boston, Little, Brown, 1963), pp. 82, 90.

25. See Charles Bell, *The Hand . . . as Evincing Design* (Philadelphia, 1836), p. 79; a representative selection from the essay appears in Jones and Cohen, pp. 37–49.

26. Charles Babbage, *The Ninth Bridgewater Treatise* (London, 1838), p. 33; this passage also appears in Jones and Cohen, p. 53.

27. William Whewell, *Astronomy and General Physics* (1833: Philadelphia, 1836), p. vii.

28. Robert Chambers, *Vestiges of Creation* (1844: New York, 1868), p. 105. This is the original wording; *Vestiges* underwent many revisions, and this passage was verbally much altered, but the meaning remained substantially the same.

29. Joule, an 1847 lecture "On Matter, Living Force and Heat," Jones and Cohen, eds., *A Treasury of Scientific Prose*, pp. 183–184.

30. See Jones and Cohen, p. 162 n.

31. Peel, *An Inaugural Address . . . Tamworth Library and Reading Room* (London, 1841), pp. 24, 28–29.

32. See, for example, Treatise VIII, William Prout, *Chemistry, Meteorology, and the Function of Digestion* (Philadelphia, 1836), the last chapter of which is summarized: "Of the Future Progress of Chemistry; of the Application of Chemistry to Physiological Research; and of the Tendency of Physical Knowledge to Elevate the Mind by Displaying the Attributes of the Deity and the Immensity of His Works."

33. Newman, "The Tamworth Reading Room," C. F. Harrold, ed., *Essays and Sketches*, 3 vols. (New York, Longmans, 1948), II, 208, 209, 211, 212.

34. Quoted by C. F. Harrold, *John Henry Newman* (New York, Longmans, 1945), p. 352, from Wilfrid Ward, *Life of Cardinal Newman*, 2 vols. (London, Longmans, 1912), II, 81.

35. Contrast the warm emotion of the Bridgewater Treatises with the cooler "scientific" tone of Maxwell's first paper on electricity, read to the Cambridge Philosophical Society in December 1855 (reprinted in part by Jones and Cohen, eds., *A Treasury of Scientific Prose*, pp. 327–335), where the conclusion of the general remarks runs: "If the results of mere speculation which I have collected are found to be of any use to experimental philosophers, in arranging and interpreting their results, they will have served their purpose, and a mature theory, in which physical facts will be physically explained, will be formed by those who by interrogating Nature herself can obtain the only true solution of the questions which the mathematical theory suggests."

36. Arnold, "Theodore Parker" (1867), *Culture and Anarchy, with . . . Some Literary Essays*, R. H. Super, ed., *Complete Prose Works*, V (Ann Arbor, University of Michigan Press, 1965), 83.

37. Seeley, *Ecce Homo*, p. 353.

38. Francis Darwin, ed., *Life and Letters of Charles Darwin*, 2 vols. (New York, 1887), II, 56. The sentence is also quoted in a valuable article by John C. Greene, "Evolution and Progress," *The Johns Hopkins Magazine*, XIV (1962), 8–12, 32.

39. T. H. Huxley, *Evolution and Ethics, Selected Works*, Westminster Edition, p. 85.

40. Herbert Spencer, *Social Statics* (New York, 1882), p. 80. This book first appeared in 1850, nine years before *The Origin of Species*, but Spencer's later volumes amplify rather than negate the idea of progress here presented; cf., for example, his *Illustrations of Universal Progress* (New York, 1864).

41. Julian Huxley, *Man in the Modern World* (New York, New American Library, 1948), p. 176; see also his *Evolution in Action* (1953) and *The Humanist Frame* (1962), which he edited.

42. Bertrand Russell, *Has Man a Future?* (London, Penguin Books, 1961), pp. 121, 127. The notion of predictable progeny is most clearly associated with the American geneticist Hermann Muller.

43. Wordsworth, "Answer to the Letter of 'Mathetes,·'" in *The Friend*, 1809, A. B. Grosart, ed., *Prose Works*, 3 vols. (London, 1876), I, 322.

CHAPTER IV. THE RECESSION OF PROGRESS

1. Hallam, Lord Tennyson's account of his father's opinion, *Alfred, Lord Tennyson: A Memoir*, 2 vols. (New York, 1897), II, 329.

2. Henry George, *Progress and Poverty* (1879: New York, Schalkenbach, 1937), pp. 6, 7, 8, 10, 286. There were ten English editions of this book by 1884.

3. See John Morley, *Politics and History* (London, Macmillan, 1923), p. 74.

4. Morley, *On Compromise*, p. 23, and *Politics and History*, p. 75.

5. Huxley, "Evolution and Ethics" (1893), *Evolution and Ethics*, p. 78.

6. Harrison, *The Choice of Books*, p. 443.

7. Huxley, "The Struggle for Existence in Human Society," *Evolution and Ethics*, p. 199.

8. See Glyn Daniel, *The Idea of Prehistory*, pp. 57–59. Dr. Daniel raises the important question of whether the Victorian archaeologist was being objective when he assumed progress or decay: "was he making an objective archaeological evaluation which enabled prehistory to confirm the Victorian idea of progress, or was he projecting into prehistory his own widely shared ideas of progress?" and, again, was the later concern with regression more than "a late Victorian defeatism projected into the archaeological record?" (p. 60).

9. Gordon Haight, ed., *The George Eliot Letters*, III, 227–228.

10. Harrison, *The Choice of Books*, p. 436.

11. Alfred North Whitehead, *Science and the Modern World* (New York, Macmillan, 1947), p. 148.

12. Ruskin, *Modern Painters*, *Works*, V, 327.

13. Conrad, quoted by Eloise Knapp Hay, *The Political Novels of Joseph Conrad* (Chicago, University of Chicago Press, 1963), pp. 172–175.

14. An early passage from the manuscript of *The Rescue*, quoted by Mrs. Hay, p. 106. Some of the late nineteenth-century eugenists argued, in terms very like those of Travers, that progress demanded that we the strong should destroy the weak and the defective; see, for a frightening example, W. Duncan McKim, *Heredity and Human Progress* (New York, Putnam, 1900), in which the author insists that there can be "no nobler, no tenderer charity than the methodic but gentle extinction of the very weak and the very vicious."

15. Bury's summary of Comte's three stages, *The Idea of Progress*, p. 292.

16. Letter of August 1895 to Lady Burne-Jones, Philip Henderson, ed., *The Letters of William Morris to his Family and Friends* (London, Longmans, 1950), p. 374.

17. Arnold, *Culture and Anarchy* (1869), Super, ed., *Prose Works*, V, 103–104.

18. Ruskin, "Fiction—Fair and Foul" (1880), *Works*, XXXIV, 266.

19. Arnold, "The Future" (1852).

20. Arnold, *Culture and Anarchy, Prose Works*, V, 108.

21. Arnold, "The Function of Criticism at the Present Time" (1864), Super, ed., *Prose Works*, III (Ann Arbor, University of Michigan Press, 1962), 269.

22. Carlyle, *Heroes and Hero-Worship, Works*, V, 118.

23. See Albert J. Guerard, ed., *Hardy: A Collection of Critical Essays* (Englewood Cliffs, N. J., Prentice-Hall, 1963), editor's introduction, p. 6.

24. *Jude the Obscure*, Part VI, Chapters II, X.

25. Ruskin, *Modern Painters, Works*, V, 380–381.

CHAPTER V. THE IDEA OF DECADENCE

1. G. Jean-Aubry, ed., *The Works of Joseph Conrad: Life and Letters*, 2 vols. (New York, Doubleday, 1928), I, 222.

2. Sir William Thomson (Lord Kelvin), *Mathematical and Physical Papers*, 5 vols. (Cambridge, England, 1882–1911), I, 514; reprinted from *Proceedings of the Royal Society of Edinburgh*, April 19, 1852.

3. Balfour Stewart, *The Conservation of Energy* (London, 1873), p. 153. For an earlier and somewhat less popular comment on the second law of thermodynamics, see Hermann von Helmholtz, "On the Interaction of Natural Forces," *The Correlation and Conservation of Forces* (New York, 1865), E. L. Youmans, ed., p. 229: "At all events, we must admire the sagacity of Thomson, who, in the letters of a long known little mathematical formula, which only speaks of the heat, volume and pressure of bodies, was able to discern consequences which threatened the universe, though certainly after an infinite period of time, with eternal death." (But Thomson, we remember, spoke of "a finite period" of time.)

4. Brooks Adams, *The Law of Civilization and Decay* (London, 1895), p. 292; see also prefatory remarks, p. viii: "In this last stage

of consolidation, the economic, and perhaps, the scientific intellect is propagated, while the imagination fades, and the emotional, the martial, and the artistic types of manhood decay."

5. Letter quoted in preface to Henry Adams, *The Degradation of the Democratic Dogma*, pp. 98–99.

6. Ruskin, "Deucalion" (1875), *Works*, XXVI, 117, 123.

7. See, for example, Ruskin's strange, half-mad lecture of 1884, *The Storm Cloud of the Nineteenth Century*, based in part on accurate meteorological observations (recorded in his notebooks over long years) and in part on his obsession that the moral darkness of the modern world was being written on the heavens.

8. Huxley, "Evolution and Ethics, Prolegomena" (1894), *Evolution and Ethics*, p. 43.

9. Balfour, *Decadence* (Cambridge, England, Cambridge University Press, 1908), p. 34.

10. See P. H. Newby's introduction to his edition of *Eothen* (London, Lehmann, 1948), p. v.

11. Macaulay's 1840 review of Ranke's *History of the Popes*, *Essays*, II², 301.

12. Froude, "The Science of History," *Short Studies on Great Subjects* (New York, 1868), p. 35.

13. Ruskin, *Fors Clavigera*, Letter 67 (July 1876), *Works*, XXVIII, 638.

14. Hopkins, "Tom's Garland," sonnet of September 1887, *Poems*, p. 108, and Hopkins's comment to Bridges (February 1888), quoted in note to the poem, p. 247.

15. Morris, *News from Nowhere*, p. 164.

16. Letter of May 1885, in Henderson, ed., *Letters of Morris*, p. 236.

17. Morris mentions *After London* in a letter of April 1885, a fortnight before his comment on barbarism; see Henderson, p. 236.

18. Richard Jefferies, *After London; or, Wild England* (1885: London, 1886), p. 69.

19. I have here drawn rather heavily on my own discussion of *Idylls of the King* in *Tennyson: the Growth of a Poet* (Cambridge, Harvard University Press, 1960), pp. 171–194.

20. Cf. A. E. Carter's able and suggestive study, *The Idea of Decadence in French Literature* (Toronto, University of Toronto Press, 1958), pp. 144–145, and on the sanctions of the idea in France, pp. 148–149.

21. Thomson, *England in the Nineteenth Century*, p. 165. I am indebted to this book for several of my generalizations about the

economy, and also to R. C. K. Ensor, *England, 1870–1914* (Oxford, Oxford University Press, 1936). See also J. H. Clapham, *An Economic History of Modern Britain*, 2 vols. (Cambridge, England, Cambridge University Press, 1926, 1932), vol. II.

22. Havelock Ellis, *The New Spirit* (1890: Boston, Houghton Mifflin, 1926), pp. 24, 25.

23. Arnold Toynbee and Philip Toynbee, *Comparing Notes: A Dialogue across a Generation* (London, Weidenfeld Nicolson, 1963), p. 83.

24. Henley, "Epilogue" (1901) to *For England's Sake, Works*, II, 159.

25. Gladstone, "England's Mission," *Nineteenth Century*, IV (1878), 581.

26. Ruskin, "Of Modern Landscape," *Modern Painters, Works*, V, 321–322.

27. Though Nietzsche would not have considered himself a pessimist, his impatience with traditional values, his bitter wit, his contempt for unaesthetic democracy were scarcely "optimistic" in the usual sense of that word.

28. R. M. Wenley, *Aspects of Pessimism* (Edinburgh, 1894), p. 250.

29. Albert Schweitzer, *The Decay and Restoration of Civilization* (1922: London, Black, 1947), p. 15.

30. See Oswald Spengler, *The Decline of the West*, 2 vols. (1926, 1928: New York, Knopf, 1950), esp. II, 90–155, on the megalopolis; and I, 183 f., on the Faustian soul. For a succinct estimate of Spengler's message and significance, see H. Stuart Hughes, *Oswald Spengler* (New York, Scribner, 1952).

31. Harry T. Moore, ed., *The Collected Letters of D. H. Lawrence*, 2 vols. (New York, Viking, 1962), I, 481–482, II, 905.

32. Hardy, "Apology," *Late Lyrics and Earlier* (London, Macmillan, 1922), p. xiv. Hardy sees—oddly enough, in view of his earlier hostility to organized religion—some forlorn hope in the English Church, almost all that is "left in this country to keep the shreds of morality together," and the chance that the Church will effect some working alliance between the religious spirit and scientific rationality.

33. Osbert Sitwell, *Laughter in the Next Room* (Boston, Little Brown, 1948), p. 366.

34. Wyndham Lewis, *The Demon of Progress in the Arts* (London, Methuen, 1954), p. 96.

35. Herbert Read, writing in 1962, *The Contrary Experience* (London, Faber, 1963), p. 11.

36. Cf. Chad Walsh, *From Utopia to Nightmare* (New York, Harper, 1962). Mr. Walsh traces the decline of utopian literature partly to the fact that many of the objectives of the Victorian socialists had already been achieved by the early twentieth century and partly to the presence of new violence, brutality, and totalitarian regimentation.

37. Wells, *The Fate of Man* (New York, Longmans, 1939), p. 246.

38. Wells, *Mind at the End of its Tether* (London, Heinemann, 1945), pp. 1, 4, 9, 17, 18. See also Antonina Vallentin's account of Wells's last years in her *H. G. Wells* (New York, Day, 1950), pp. 310–326.

39. The context (George is speaking of the childless women in the story) suggests that Wells may have had the play in mind, for Granville-Barker had made sterility and abortion the signs and symbols of decadence. Wells appeared in the role of Gilbert Wedgecroft, when *Waste* was produced for purposes of stage copyright at the Savoy Theatre on January 28, 1908.

40. Pater, *The Renaissance*, p. 87; the phrase occurs in the essay on Leonardo da Vinci; cf. the reference, in the "Preface," to "that subtle and delicate sweetness which belongs to a refined and comely decadence" (p. xxix).

41. Rémy de Gourmont, *Decadence and Other Essays on the Culture of Ideas* (New York, Harcourt-Brace, 1921), p. 142.

42. Ruskin, *The Two Paths, Works*, XVI, 342.

43. Herbert Read, "The Symptoms of Decadence," *To Hell with Culture* (London, Routledge, 1963), p. 91.

44. See Carter, *The Idea of Decadence in French Literature*, p. 145.

45. Andrew Lang, "Decadence," *Critic*, XXXVII (1900), 171–173.

46. R. W. Dixon, quoted by J. W. Mackail, *The Life of William Morris*, 2 vols. (London, Longmans, 1912), I, 48.

47. Pater, "Style," *Appreciations* (1889: London, Macmillan, 1931), p. 13.

48. But it can be argued that Tennyson's lavish expenditures in style did actually bring a main poetic tradition to the verge of bankruptcy; see the provocative article by A. J. Carr, "Tennyson as a Modern Poet," *University of Toronto Quarterly*, XIX (1950), 361–382. On the larger issue of the possible exhaustion of literary

subject matter, as it perplexed eighteenth-century and Romantic writers, see W. J. Bate, "The English Poet and the Burden of the Past, 1660-1820," Earl R. Wasserman, ed., *Aspects of the Eighteenth Century* (Baltimore, The Johns Hopkins Press, 1965), pp. 245-264.

49. Pater, "Conclusion," *The Renaissance*, p. 195. Cf. C. E. M. Joad's definition, in his *Decadence* (New York, Philosophical Library, 1949), p. 54: "Decadence is identified with the valuing of experience for its own sake, irrespective of the quality of the experience, the object of experience, that upon which the experience is, as it were directed, being left out of account. Decadence, then, is defined as 'the dropping of the object.'"

50. Wilde, "The Critic as Artist" (1890), Richard Aldington, ed., *The Portable Oscar Wilde* (New York, Viking, 1946), p. 113.

51. See Carter, p. 149; and on the French Decadents, see also George Ross Ridge, *The Hero in French Decadent Literature* (Athens, Georgia, University of Georgia Press, 1961).

52. Mallarmé, quoted by Jacques Letheve, "Le Thème de la décadence dans les lettres françaises à la fin du XIXe siècle," *Revue d'histoire littéraire de la France*, LXIII (1963), 48.

53. Francis Bacon in an interview, *Sunday Times* (London) *Magazine*, July 14, 1963, p. 13.

54. Wilde, "The Critic as Artist," p. 103.

CHAPTER VI. THE PASSION OF THE PAST

1. Stevenson, "In the States," December 1879, published 1887; "Sing Me a Song," written about 1887. For the dating, see Janet Adam Smith, ed., *Robert Louis Stevenson: Collected Poems* (London, Hart-Davis, 1948), pp. 483, 517. As the adaptation of an older folk lyric, "Sing Me a Song" is clearly less personal in origin than "In the States," but it has nonetheless, I believe, a strong subjective overtone.

2. Cf. Hans Meyerhoff, *Time in Literature*, pp. 29-32. "What we are," Meyerhoff remarks, "we are only in and through time; but we are constantly changed in and by time." How, then, can we "dip into the same river of our own selves, whether past or present, if the moments we catch are always different?"

3. Pater, "Conclusion," *The Renaissance*, p. 196.

4. Wordsworth, *The Prelude* (1850), Book I, lines 620-625; Book XII, lines 269-271.

5. *The Mill on the Floss*, Book VII, Chapter V; *Great Expectations*, Chapter LVI. In "Brother and Sister," an apparently autobiographical poem dated 1869, George Eliot explicitly designates past impressions as her "root of piety":

> The wide-arched bridge, the scented elder-flowers,
> The wondrous watery rings that died too soon,
> The echoes of the quarry, the still hours
> With white robe sweeping on the shadeless noon,
>   Were but my growing self, are part of me,
>   My present Past, my root of piety.

6. *The Prelude*, Book I, lines 344–350.

7. Letter to Sir George Beaumont, May 1, 1805, Ernest de Selincourt, ed., *The Early Letters of William and Dorothy Wordsworth* (Oxford, Oxford University Press, 1935), p. 489.

8. Edward Sackville-West, ed., *Confessions of an English Opium-Eater* (London, Cresset Press, 1950), p. 291.

9. Though not published till 1911, Harrison's *Autobiographic Memoirs* may properly, in view of its tone and substance, be considered a "Victorian" work; so may Morley's *Recollections*, which did not appear till 1917.

10. Anthony Trollope, *An Autobiography* (1883: Berkeley, University of California Press, 1947), p. 304.

11. John, Viscount Morley, *Recollections*, 2 vols. (New York, Macmillan, 1917), p. ix.

12. See Henri-A. Talon's fine essay, "Time and Memory in Thackeray's *Henry Esmond*," *Review of English Studies*, XIII (1962), 147–156. Swinburne's poetic autobiography "Thalassius," published in 1880, is also written in the third person.

13. A. Dwight Culler, ed., *Apologia pro Vita Sua* (Boston, Houghton Mifflin, 1956), pp. 18–19. The second edition (1865) was titled *History of My Religious Opinions*, but in 1873 Newman returned to the original title, *Apologia pro Vita Sua*, and added the subtitle, *Being a History of his Religious Opinions*.

14. Nora Barlow, ed., *The Autobiography of Charles Darwin* (New York, Harcourt Brace, 1959), p. 21; the passage is dated May 31, 1876. Cf. the opening of Frederick Locker-Lampson's *My Confidences* (London, 1896): "In the dim vistas of memory, . . . my life seems like a dream, lagging, yet fleeting; so vague that it might almost have been lived or dreamt by somebody else."

15. John Stuart Mill, *Autobiography* (1873: New York, Columbia University Press, 1924), p. 1.

16. Mill's autobiography as published does not once mention his mother; an early draft of the manuscript, however, cited by Michael St. John Packe, dismissed her as a cold-hearted woman who brought no love to her family. See Packe, *The Life of John Stuart Mill*, p. 33.

17. Ruskin, *Praeterita, Works*, XXV, 11.

18. Hazlitt, "On the Feeling of Immortality in Youth," *Complete Works*, 21 vols. (London, Dent, 1933), XVII, 199.

19. De Quincey, "The Pains of Opium," *Confessions*, pp. 328–329.

20. Ruskin, "Pre-Raphaelitism," *Works*, XII, 360.

21. Samuel Butler, *Unconscious Memory* (London, 1880), p. 272.

22. Pater, *Marius the Epicurean*, Chapters VII, IX.

23. *David Copperfield*, Chapter XI. Dickens indeed transcribed this sentence almost word for word from the autobiographical fragment he gave John Forster; see Forster, who quotes the unpublished passage, *The Life of Charles Dickens*, 3 vols. (Philadelphia, 1873), I, 53. Forster comments (I, 49) on the fragment: "It had all been written, as fact, before he thought of any other use for it; and it was not until several months later, when the fancy of *David Copperfield*, itself suggested by what he had so written of his early troubles, began to take shape in his mind, that he abandoned the intention of writing his own life. Those warehouse experiences fell then so aptly into the subject he had chosen, that he could not resist the temptation of immediately using them." But it is unlikely that Dickens would ever have published so painful and private a confession without the protective framework of fiction.

24. *The Ordeal of Richard Feverel*, Chapter XXI.

25. Allingham, *Poems* (London, Macmillan, 1912), p. 65.

26. Burne-Jones, quoted by Georgiana Burne-Jones, *Memorials of Edward Burne-Jones*, 2 vols. (New York, Macmillan, 1904), I, 151.

27. Hardy, "Under the Waterfall," *Satires of Circumstance* (1914), *Collected Poems*, p. 315. The poem goes on to describe the sensation as "a throe / From the past [which] awakens a sense of that time."

28. *David Copperfield*, Chapters XXVI, LX. My attention was called to these passages by J. Hillis Miller's stimulating discussion of *David Copperfield* as a novel of memory in his *Charles Dickens: The World of his Novels* (Cambridge, Harvard University Press, 1958), pp. 152–158. Mr. Miller also makes a distinction between Dickens and Proust. The scent of the geranium leaf anticipates

the odor of currants in *Great Expectations* (Chapter XIX), where Biddy crushes a leaf as she tries to make herself understood by the impercipient Pip: "Biddy, having rubbed the leaf to pieces between her hands,—and the smell of a black-currant bush has ever since recalled to me that evening in the garden by the side of the lane—said . . ."

29. *David Copperfield*, Chapter XXXIX.

30. Tennyson, *Memoir*, I, 253. For a general discussion of the place of "mystical" experience in Tennyson's development, see my *Tennyson: The Growth of a Poet*, esp. pp. 14–19, 122–124, 188–189. Relevant poems to consider, in addition to *In Memoriam* and "The Ancient Sage," include "Armageddon," "The Mystic," "The Two Voices," "The Holy Grail," "De Profundis," and "Far —Far—Away."

31. William Empson, *English Pastoral Poetry* (New York, Norton, 1938), pp. 270–271.

32. See Robert Lee Wolff, *The Golden Key* (New Haven, Yale University Press, 1961).

33. *Marius*, Chapter XXVII.

34. "The Door in the Wall," published first in 1906, later appeared in *The Country of the Blind* (1911).

35. "The Holy Grail," lines 901–905.

36. Macaulay, quoted by John Clive in his perceptive article, "Macaulay's Historical Imagination," *Review of English Literature*, I (1960), 23.

CHAPTER VII. THE LIVING PRESENT

1. Hardy, "Going and Staying," *Collected Poems*, p. 543.

2. Ruskin, letter to Mrs. Browning in November 1856, *Works*, XXVI, 247; also cited by Derrick Leon, *Ruskin* (London, Routledge, 1949), p. 243.

3. Ruskin, quoted by Hallam Tennyson, *Memoir*, I, 453.

4. George Eliot, *Essays and Leaves from a Notebook* (New York, 1884), pp. 290–291.

5. George Eliot, "Looking Backward," *Impressions of Theophrastus Such* (New York, n.d.), p. 26.

6. Macaulay, *History of England*, 3 vols. (New York, 1880), I, 2.

7. See Bertrand Russell, "The Guardians of Parnassus," *Satan in the Suburbs* (London, Penguin Books, 1963), p. 127.

8. Ruskin, "Of Modern Landscape," *Modern Painters*, III, *Works*, V, 326.

9. The last paragraph of *Hypatia* (1853), where Kingsley spells out the moral of the tale.

10. See Curtis Dahl, "History on the Hustings: Bulwer Lytton's Historical Novels of Politics," in Robert C. Rathburn and Martin Steinmann, Jr., eds., *From Jane Austen to Joseph Conrad* (Minneapolis, University of Minnesota Press, 1958), pp. 60–71; Professor Dahl makes interesting comments on Bulwer's *Harold* and *Rienzi* as well as *The Last of the Barons*.

11. Cf. Robert Kiely, *Robert Louis Stevenson and the Fiction of Adventure* (Cambridge, Harvard University Press, 1964), p. 233: "In fact, the basic theme of the novel is that the crude energies of the heroic past continually inform and affect contemporary life."

12. Arnold, "The Function of Criticism at the Present Time" (1864), Super, ed., *Prose Works*. III, 285.

13. Super, ed., *Prose Works*, V, 105.

14. So he told his wife; see David Alec Wilson, *Carlyle on Cromwell and Others* (London, Kegan Paul, 1925), p. 181.

15. Letter of August 29, 1842, quoted by Wilson, p. 182.

16. "Signs of the Times" appeared in the *Edinburgh Review* for June 1829; its title was drawn from Matthew 16:3, "O ye hypocrites, ye can discern the face of the sky; but can ye not discern the signs of the times?"

17. Ruskin, *Praeterita, Works*, XXXV, 391.

18. William Michael Rossetti, ed., *Dante Gabriel Rossetti: his Family-Letters with a Memoir*, 2 vols. (London, 1895), I, 108.

19. Rossetti, "The Choice: I," the 1870 version, considerably revised for the 1881 edition of *The House of Life;* see Paull Franklin Baum, ed., *The House of Life* (Cambridge, Harvard University Press, 1928), p. 176.

20. On the discovery of *The Rubáiyát* by Whitley Stokes, who called it to Rossetti's attention, see Carl J. Weber's Centennial Edition of the poem (Waterville, Maine, Colby College Press, 1959), pp. 17–22.

21. *Pendennis*, Chapter 61; also quoted by Gordon N. Ray, *Thackeray: The Age of Wisdom* (New York, McGraw-Hill, 1958), p. 120. Mr. Ray comments that this "Sadduceeism" or "general scepticism" seemed to Thackeray "the only rational attitude."

22. D. H. Lawrence, letter of March 9, 1916, *Letters*, I, 442.

23. Browning, "Saul," lines 78–79. The speaker is, of course,

David, but the sentiment accords well with Browning's own as it appears in many nondramatic lyrics.

24. Hopkins, "To his Watch," *Poems*, p. 166.

25. Two of these ecstatic poems, "The Starlight Night" and "Pied Beauty," are in the imperative mood, but only "The Wind-hover" employs the past tense, and then to record an almost-present observation, the flight "this morning" of the falcon, and in the sestet the past tense yields completely to the present.

26. Arthur Symons, "A Prelude to Life," *Spiritual Adventures* (London, Constable, 1905), pp. 49–50.

27. Cf. John Pick's essay on Lionel Johnson and Oscar Wilde, "Divergent Disciples of Walter Pater," *Thought*, XXIII (1948), 114–128.

28. Pater, *Marius*, Chapter IX.

29. *Marius*, Chapter IV.

30. *Marius*, Chapter XXV.

31. "Winckelmann," *The Renaissance*, pp. 192–193.

32. Arnold, "On the Modern Element in Literature," *Essays* (London, Oxford University Press, 1914), pp. 454–472, where the need of "intellectual deliverance" is made a sanction for the study of Greek literature; and a letter to Clough in H. F. Lowry, ed., *The Letters of Matthew Arnold to Arthur Hugh Clough* (New York, Oxford University Press, 1932), p. 97.

33. Pater, "Charles Lamb" (1878), *Appreciations*, p. 114. Cf. Robert Frost's "Carpe Diem" (1942).

34. F. T. Palgrave, "The Decline of Art," *Nineteenth Century*, XXIII (1888), 90.

35. Cf. Millais' unabashed confession to Holman Hunt: "For my part, I paint what there is a demand for. There is a fashion going now for little girls in mob caps. Well, I satisfy it while it continues; but immediately it shows signs of flagging, I am ready to take to some other fashion of the last century." Quoted by A. C. Gissing, *William Holman Hunt* (London, Duckworth, 1936), p. 199.

36. This is the burden of the argument of Harold A. Innis's *Changing Concepts of Time* (Toronto, University of Toronto Press, 1952); cf. esp. p. v.

37. *Marius*, Chapter XXVIII.

38. *Great Expectations*, Chapter XX.

39. Arnold, "The Function of Criticism," Super, ed., *Prose Works*, III, 272.

CHAPTER VIII. THE ETERNAL NOW

1. *David Copperfiield*, Chapter III.
2. J. Shawcross, ed., *Biographia Literaria*, 2 vols. (Oxford, Oxford University Press, 1907), II, 207.
3. Super, ed., *Prose Works of Arnold*, I, 4.
4. Richard D. Altick argues ingeniously that Browning is satirizing the grammarian and his views of life; but since the idea of eternity occurs frequently, and without irony, elsewhere in Browning, I assume that Browning does indeed feel that "Man has Forever." In any case, see Altick, " 'A Grammarian's Funeral': Browning's Praise of Folly?" *Studies in English Literature*, III (1963), 449–460.
5. Rossetti, "The Dark Glass," *The House of Life*, sonnet 34.
6. Arnold, "The Buried Life," lines 91–98.
7. Wordsworth, *The Prelude*, Book VI, lines 638–640.
8. Ruskin, *Praeterita*, *Works*, XXXV, 118. This was Ruskin's response on first seeing Milan in its mountain setting, and the context of the passage makes it clear that the city shares in the glory of the Alps: "Then the drive home in the open carriage through the quiet twilight, up the long streets, and round the base of the Duomo, the smooth pavement under the wheels adding with its silentness to the sense of dream wonder in it all,—the perfect air in absolute calm, the just seen majesty of encompassing Alps, the perfectness—so it seemed to me—and purity, of the sweet, stately, stainless marble against the sky."
9. The best general treatment of the subject remains Joseph Warren Beach's *Concept of Nature in Nineteenth Century Poetry* (New York, Macmillan, 1936).
10. *In Memoriam*, sec. LVI.
11. Arthur O'Shaughnessy, "The Line of Beauty," *Songs of a Worker* (London, 1881), p. 106.
12. See J. A. M. Whistler, "Ten O'Clock," *The Gentle Art of Making Enemies* (London, 1890).
13. C. C. Abbott, ed., *Correspondence of Gerard Manley Hopkins and Richard Watson Dixon* (New York, Oxford University Press, 1935), pp. 98–99.
14. Tennyson, *Idylls of the King*, "Gareth and Lynette," lines 222–224.
15. Ruskin, *Stones of Venice*, III, *Works*, XI, 62.

16. Pater, "The School of Giorgione," *The Renaissance*, pp. 123–124.

17. James Joyce, *Stephen Hero* (Norfolk, Connecticut, New Directions, 1963), p. 211, and *A Portrait of the Artist as a Young Man*, Harry Levin, ed., *The Portable James Joyce* (New York, Viking, 1947), p. 479.

18. Wordsworth, *The Prelude*, Book XII, lines 208–215, 249–253, and Book VI, lines 599–608.

19. Rossetti, "Silent Noon," *The House of Life*, sonnet 19.

20. Pater, *Marius*, Chapters X, XIX. There are a number of "exquisite pauses" throughout the novel: e.g., the passage describing the snakes (Chapter II), the death of Flavian (VII), Marius's noticing the indifference of Marcus Aurelius to the cruelty of the gladiatorial combat (XIV).

21. George Eliot, *Daniel Deronda*, Chapter XL. Mordecai later (Chapter XLIII) describes another epiphany, a crucial moment of his youth when on the quay at Trieste, "where the ground I stood on seemed to send forth light, and the shadows had an azure glory as of spirits become visible, I felt myself in the flood of a glorious life, wherein my own small year-counted existence seemed to melt, so that I knew it not: and a great sob arose within me as at the rush of waters that were too strong a bliss."

22. Conrad, *Lord Jim*, Chapter XXIII. In *The Arrow of Gold* (Part Two, I) the narrator's first sight of Doña Rita brings another and quite Paterian epiphany; and the lady herself, who seems to have in her "something of the women of all time," is strongly reminiscent of Pater's Mona Lisa, in that she is a composite and a quintessence: her face "drew irresistibly your gaze to itself by an indefinable quality of charm beyond all analysis and made you think of remote races, of strange generations, of the faces of women sculptured on immemorial monuments and of those lying unsung in their tombs." The total impression at this exquisite moment is, we are told, one of "absolute harmony."

23. Virginia Woolf, *A Room of One's Own* (New York, Harcourt, Brace, 1929), pp. 191–192.

24. Rossetti, quoted by Hall Caine, *Recollections of Rossetti* (Boston, 1883), p. 201.

25. For the anecdote, see Helen Rossetti Angeli, *Dante Gabriel Rossetti, his Friends and Enemies* (London, Hamilton, 1949), p. 254.

26. Hall Caine, p. 201.

27. On Rossetti's reaction to Buchanan, see J. A. Cassidy, "Robert Buchanan and the Fleshly Controversy," *PMLA*, LXVII (1952), 65–93, and on his relation to aestheticism, Buckley, *The Victorian Temper*, pp. 161–171.

28. Kipling, "Cities and Thrones and Powers," *Puck of Pook's Hill* (1906).

29. Tennyson, "The Ancient Sage," lines 103–105.

INDEX

Abbott, C. C., 177
Acland, Henry, 161
Acton, Lord, 23–24, 29, 40, 42
Adams, Brooks, 68; *Law of Civilization and Decay*, 68, 167–168
Adams, Henry, 10, 67–68, 100
Adderley, Sir Charles, 135
Aeschylus, 123
Aesthetic Movement, 19
Ainger, A. C., 163
Albert, Prince Consort, 35
Aldington, Richard, 171
Allingham, William, 106
Altholz, Josef, L., 160
Altick, Richard D., 177
Ancients and Moderns, Quarrel of, 39
Angeli, Helen Rossetti, 178
Antiquaries, Society of, 29
Arkwright, Richard, 10
Arnold, Matthew, viii, 3, 12, 17, 18, 46–47, 52, 57, 61–62, 75–78, 89, 118, 122–123, 133, 134, 135–136, 139, 141–142, 144; *Balder Dead*, 17; *Culture and Anarchy*, 123; "Dover Beach," 57; *Empedocles on Etna*, 77, 123, 139; "The Function of Criticism at the Present Time," 77, 121, 122–123; Marguerite lyrics, 99; "Memorial Verses," 75–76; "The New Sirens," 122; "Progress," 62; "Revolutions," 76; "Saint Brandon," 17; "The Scholar-Gypsy," 12, 144; "Sohrab and Rustum," 17; *Tristram and Iseult*, 17, 144; "The Youth of Nature," 76
Arnold, Dr. Thomas, 41
art nouveau, 143
autobiography, 97–102

Babbage, Charles, 44
Bacon, Francis, 26; *The New Atlantis*, 26; Baconian method, 26, 35

Bacon, Francis (painter), 171
Bagehot, Walter, 41
Balfour, A. J., 70–71
Barbey d'Aurevilly, 90
Barlow, Nora, 172
Bate, W. J., 171
Baudelaire, Charles, 90; *Les Fleurs du Mal*, 90
Baum, Paull F., 175
Beach, Joseph W., 177
Beaumont, Sir George, 172
Beckett, Samuel, 86
Bell, Charles, 44
Bellamy, Edward, 86; *Looking Backward*, 86
Bentham, Jeremy, 24
Bergson, Henri, 8
Bildungsroman, 99–100
Blair, Thomas S., 163
Blunt, Wilfrid, 71
Bodichon, Barbara, 57
Bray, Mrs. Charles, 160
Bridges, Robert, 168
Bridgewater Treatises, 43–44, 45, 69, 164, 165
Browning, Elizabeth Barrett, 117, 118, 122; *Aurora Leigh*, 117, 122
Browning, Robert, 3, 17, 19, 21–22, 52, 110, 129, 130, 140–141, 177; "Abt Vogler," 117; "A Grammarian's Funeral," 141, 177; "The Last Ride Together," 147; "Never the Time and the Place," 110; "Rabbi Ben Ezra," 52, 140–141
Buchanan, Robert, *The Fleshly School of Poetry*, 152
Buckle, H. T., 30, 40
Buckley, J. H., 159, 168, 174, 179
Bulwer, Edward (Lord Lytton), 175; *The Last of the Barons*, 121
Burne-Jones, Edward, 106
Burne-Jones, Georgiana, 167
Burton, Richard, 71

181